TOP
SECRET
FILES

PIRATES
& Buried Treasure

TOP SECRET FILES

PIRATES
& Buried Treasure

STEPHANIE BEARCE

PRUFROCK PRESS INC.
WACO, TEXAS

Library of Congress Cataloging-in-Publication Data

Bearce, Stephanie.
 Pirates and buried treasure : secrets, strange tales, and hidden facts about pirates / by
Stephanie Bearce.
   pages cm
 Includes bibliographical references.
 ISBN 978-1-61821-421-8 (pbk.)
 1. Pirates--Juvenile literature. 2. Treasure troves--Juvenile literature. I. Title.
 G535.B37 2015
 910.4'5--dc23
                    2015011444

Image credits: Page 1: *Pirate* by hunqwert/deviantart • Page 6: *Pirate Arena* by velinov/
deviantart • Page 19: *Pirate!* by NikitaCosplay/deviantart • Page 20: *Pirate England* by
MizuSasori/deviantart • Page 24: *Pirate attack* by pbario/deviantart • Page 30: *Star
Wars Pirates #1* by Brent Otey • Page 56: *Pirate* by Windfreak/deviantart • Page 96:
Ghost Ship by NooA/deviantart

Prufrock Press Inc.
P.O. Box 8813
Waco, TX 76714-8813
Phone: (800) 998-2208
Fax: (800) 240-0333
http://www.prufrock.com

Table of Contents

VIPs
(Very Important Pirates)

Pirate's Treasure

Warning!

Halt ye landlubbers! Don't ye read any further unless you've a strong stomach and curious mind. These pirate stories be sometimes scary and sometimes gruesome, but they all be true.

And the truth can be a very frightening thing!

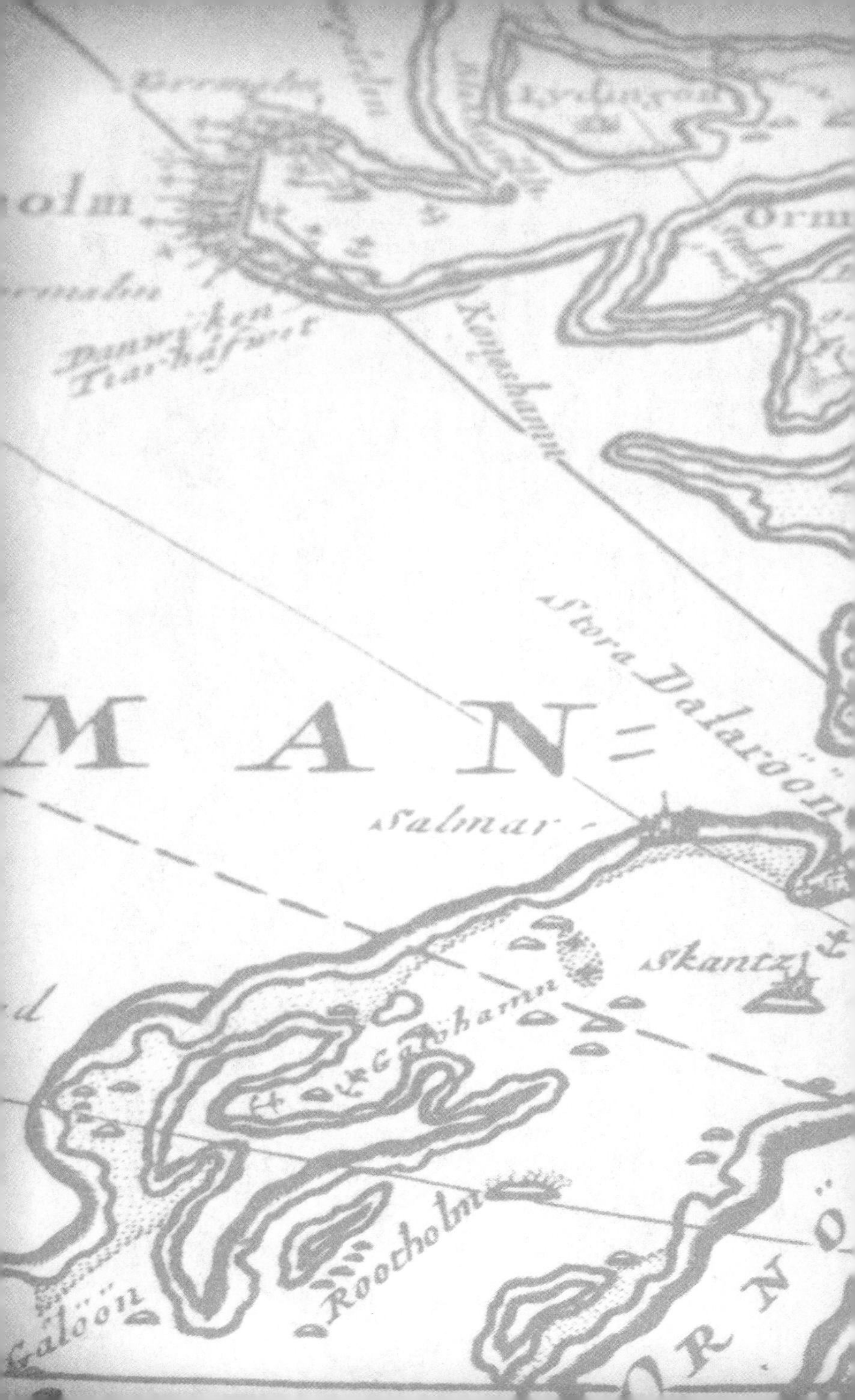
M A N
Stora Dalaröön
Salmar
Skantz
Roocholm

Pirate Problems

A Pirate's Life for Me?

Pirating sounds like a grand life. Sailing on the warm sunny seas just looking for the next ship that could be filled with treasure. Fighting your enemies and earning piles of gold and jewels. And you don't need a bank because you can just bury your plunder, make a map, and come back for it later after you're tired of salt water and sandy beaches.

The true life of a pirate was actually very short and hard. Most people who became pirates were either killed in battles or were caught and hanged. Some of the pirates, like Blackbeard, had their heads cut off and put on public display to warn other people not to go into the pirate business. After Captain Kidd was hanged, his body was covered in tar and hung by chains along the Thames River. Other pirates like François l'Olonnais made big mistakes like landing on an island inhabited by cannibals. L'Olonnais and his crew were invited to dinner—as the main course.

Daily life on a pirate ship was full of hard work. Sailors had to hoist heavy ropes, move wet heavy canvas, scrub decks, clean and care for guns and weapons, and of course, sail the ship. Sometimes their lives were quite boring. For weeks, they saw nothing but a vast empty ocean and there was very little entertainment. When they weren't working, they might play cards, tell stories, sing songs, or try to take a nap. But there were no televisions, game systems, or phones, and most pirates couldn't even read, so no books.

When pirates did get a chance to rest, it wasn't in a bed. They slept in hammocks slung above one another in the dark, damp hull of the ship. Some of the men hated sleeping inside the ship because of the terrible smell of rotting sewage and body odor. They would rather sleep on the deck of the ship and deal with the bad weather than sleep inside. Usually, the only person on the ship who had a bed was the captain. But even his bed was full of lice and bedbugs.

Pirates didn't have bathtubs or showers and not much soap. Cleanliness was not a priority for pirates. So, it was pretty smelly on the pirate ship. It was also one of the reasons so many died of diseases. If a pirate got hurt, the wound would easily become infected with dirt and germs. Pirates and other sailors often died from blood poisoning or tetanus. They also died from dysentery (extreme diarrhea), smallpox, pneumonia, and scurvy.

Scurvy was a disease caused by lack of vitamin C. Before the days of refrigeration and canning, there was no way for ships to keep fresh fruits and vegetables. Pirates went weeks without any fruits or vegetables, eating just dried meats and stale crackers. The pirates knew they had scurvy when their gums would bleed, their teeth fell out, and their legs began to turn black. Hundreds of sailors and pirates died from scurvy every year. When they died, their bodies were simply thrown overboard.

FRANCOIS LOLONOIS.
geboren in Olonne in Vrankryk,
Generaal van de Franse Rovers in Tortuga

If life at sea was so hard, why would anyone want to become a pirate? Because life as a common sailor was even worse. Sailors in the Royal Navy and Merchant Marine suffered all of the same problems as pirates, but also worked for little or no pay. And many of the sailors never even wanted to go to sea. They were captured by members of press gangs and forced to become sailors against their will.

Because life at sea was so hard, the navy had a difficult time getting enough people to staff their ships. The navy hired men, called press gangs, who would roam the countryside looking for young men who were fit and able-bodied. They would literally kidnap the men, often out of a pub, and lock them in the hold of the ship until the ship had set sail and was far from shore. Then the men were forced to go to work as sailors because there was no way to escape other than drowning. The press gangs were paid by the ship's owners for each man they could press into service.

Many of the men were virtually slaves, with their only hope of freedom coming when the ship returned back to England. If a young man who lived near the coast turned up missing, his family usually suspected kidnapping by a press gang. Some families never heard from their sons again. Lucky families might see their son again in 3 years if he survived the voyage and was released from his impressment.

When pirates raided ships, many of the sailors volunteered to join the pirate crew. On a pirate ship, the crew split their plunder equally and every crewman got a share. At least they had a hope of being paid and a chance of living a free life.

Some people volunteered to become pirates because they had "learned the ropes" (how to run the ship's rigging) on a navy vessel and thought they could earn a better living on a pirate ship. Some of the sailors were sick of being treated badly by their navy captains and "jumped ship," meaning they left the navy ship and snuck onto a pirate ship. They hoped to be treated better by the pirate captain. And many sailors did find that the pirate captain allowed them a vote and a say in the running of the ship. It was better than their life as an ordinary sailor.

In the 1700s, the life of a sailor was so dismal that famous British author Samuel Johnson said:

> "No man will be a sailor who has contrivance enough to get himself into a jail; for being in a ship is being in a jail, with the chance of being drowned . . . a man in a jail has more room, better food, and commonly better company."

SET SAIL!

If you want to learn more about the everyday life of a pirate, watch this video created by history.com. But be warned—it's got some gross information!

http://www.history.com/videos/life-aboard-a-pirate-ship#life-aboard-a-pirate-ship

Pirate Jobs and Rules

Most people imagine that life aboard a pirate ship was full of fistfights, sword battles, knife games, and drinking. But a ship that was full of that much chaos would never be organized enough to attack another vessel. Pirates realized that they had to have some form of regulation so they could work together, or they would never succeed.

The navies of the late 1600s and early 1700s were strictly controlled by a chain of command. Whatever the captain of the ship ordered had to be carried out with no questions asked. Punishments were extremely harsh, even for minor offenses. If a sailor was caught stealing, he would be flogged with a cat o' nine tails. This was a whip with nine knotted thongs designed to create as much pain as possible. For more serious crimes, there was keelhauling, where a sailor was tied to a rope looped beneath the vessel. Then the sailor was drug underneath the ship. His skin was ripped apart from the barnacles on the ship's hull.

Many sailors did not trust the captain of the ship, with good reason. Many captains were the sons or nephews of wealthy men. These captains had very little knowledge of ships and no real leadership experience. The only way they could keep control of the ship was with the threat of punishment. This led to some great disasters. Bad captains caused ships to crash into rocks, sink in storms, and lose in battle.

The only way navy sailors could get rid of a bad captain was to organize a mutiny, where all of the sailors would agree to kill, imprison, or maroon the captain. Once the old captain was out of the way, the next highest ranking officer would take over. The crew had to hope this new captain would be better. And if the crew dared to return to shore, they still had to deal with the rules, which said that mutiny aboard a Royal Navy ship was punishable by imprisonment or death.

Many pirates were former sailors and they wanted nothing to do with a ship that was run like the navy. Other pirates were former slaves or indentured servants who had suffered abuse at the hands of plantation owners. They did not want to work for a captain who would treat them the same way as the slave owners. The pirate's solution was one of democracy. Pirate officers were elected by a majority vote.

The captain on a pirate ship knew that he could be replaced at any time. If he was not aggressive enough in attacking ships or if he didn't capture enough money, prizes, and goods, then the crew would simply vote him out. A captain would also be sacked if he were too bloodthirsty and cruel. When the captain was voted out, he was then given a choice to join the crew or be set ashore.

The names of the crew leaders on a pirate ship were similar to those on a navy vessel but they did have different responsibilities. The captain on a pirate ship was not the supreme authority like a navy captain. He was expected to make the decisions during battle and to have a personality strong enough to hold together a crew of unruly sailors.

The quartermaster had a great deal of authority on a pirate ship. The pirates elected him to represent the interests of the crew. He was called upon to be a judge in settling onboard arguments. He determined punishments for minor offenses and kept the records for the ship. Most importantly, he decided what plunder was to be taken from a ship and divided the plunder equally between the crew. If the pirates captured a new ship, the quartermaster took over as the captain until they sold the ship or disposed of it.

The sailing master was the person in charge of navigation. He plotted the course of the ship, took care of the instruments, and read the sea charts and maps. This was a tough job and took a great deal of skill and mathematical knowledge. Many of the sailing masters on pirate ships were captured from other vessels and forced into service as a pirate—to sail the ship or die.

The boatswain was in charge of maintenance. He inspected the ship, its sails, and riggings to make sure everything was in good operating condition. It was

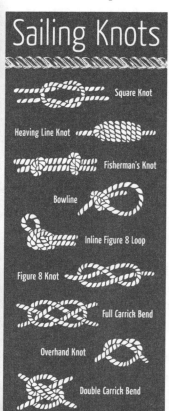

Sailing Knots

Square Knot

Heaving Line Knot

Fisherman's Knot

Bowline

Inline Figure 8 Loop

Figure 8 Knot

Full Carrick Bend

Overhand Knot

Double Carrick Bend

Where's the Grub?

Pirates often had to eat whatever they could find or catch. When at sea, pirates liked to catch sea turtles because they were full of meat. When they landed on an island, pirates would kill and eat everything from monkeys to snakes. If they were lucky, they might be able to find goats. If they were unlucky, they ate rats.

his job to meet with the captain each morning and report on the general condition of the craft. He was also in command of weighing and dropping the anchor and handling the sails.

The carpenter was a critical position because he was the man who kept the ship afloat. Wooden ships tended to rot and fall apart. The carpenter had to keep holes plugged, patch rotting timbers, and make sure the hull of the boat was scraped free of barnacles. If a pirate ship didn't have a carpenter, then they tried to capture one during their raids.

A surgeon or doctor was a luxury that most pirate ships did not have, but if they could capture one, they did. Pirates were involved in many battles and had lots of injuries that needed the attention of a surgeon. They also suffered from diseases like dysentery, malaria, and scurvy. If the pirate ship did not have a surgeon, then the carpenter would sometimes be forced to perform operations like amputations. He used the same saws to cut off limbs as he did to repair the boat.

Powder monkeys were young boys on the ship who were assigned to run gunpowder from the below decks up to the cannon crews during the battle. This was a terribly dangerous job. Those boys who survived were trained to be gunners.

The master gunner was a highly skilled position. They usually received their training in the Royal Navy. They were experts at calculating the amount of powder needed for the placement of the shot and the aim of the gun. A good master gunner could mean the difference between life and death on a pirate ship.

The truth is, life on a pirate ship had rules and order just like any good fighting unit. If there were chaos and anarchy, then the pirates would never be able to attack and conquer their quarry.

Bartholomew Roberts' crew from *The Pirates Own Book* by Charles Ellms, 1837

Bartholomew Roberts' Rules of the Ship

Below is a sample of the pirate rules on Black Bart's ship:

1. Every man shall have an equal vote in affairs of the moment. (Every person got to vote on where to sail and what ship to attack.)

2. The lights and candles shall be put out at eight at night and if any of the crew desire to drink after that hour they shall sit upon the open deck without lights. (Pirates had a curfew!)

3. None shall game for money, either with dice or cards. (Pirates weren't allowed to gamble.)

4. None shall strike another on board the ship, but every man's quarrel shall be ended onshore by sword or pistol in this manner: at the word of command from the quartermaster, each man being previously placed back to back, shall turn and fire immediately. (So no fighting on the ship. Take your duels to the shore.)

5. Each man shall keep his piece, cutlass, and pistols, at times clean and ready for action. (Pirates had to be ready for duty at all times.)

6. Every man who shall become a cripple or lose a limb in the service shall have eight hundred pieces of eight from the common stock. (Pirates tried to care for injured workmates.)

Parrots, Planks, and Maps

Everybody knows about pirates, right? A pirate is the guy with a patch over one eye and a parrot on his shoulder. He likes to attack ships, steal treasure, and make his enemies walk the plank. Oh, and he usually hides his fortune on some remote island and makes a map so he can find it again. If you think that's the truth about pirates, you better think again.

The fact is that some pirates did wear eye patches, but pirates never walked the plank and nobody has ever found a pirate's treasure map. Hollywood movies and fiction books have confused the truth about real pirates and their history. Treasure maps became a part of pirate lore after Robert Louis Stevenson wrote his famous book, *Treasure Island*. Published in 1883, this book first introduced the idea of a treasure map marked with an X. In reality, pirates did sometimes hide their loot, but they never left it for long. Pirates wanted to sell the goods and get cash as quickly as possible because they didn't want to be caught with the stolen property. Like most people of that time period, pirates were usually illiterate. They did not have the skills to create accurate maps or the ability to read a map that someone else had made.

Walking the plank was also a part of the book *Treasure Island*. There is no historical evidence that pirates actually made their captives walk a plank and plunge into the ocean, but they had lots of other nasty punishments for people they did not like, such as throwing people overboard or hanging them.

Eye patches were a fact for many pirates, but not because they had an eye poked out. It is believed that pirates wore eye patches to help their eyes adjust to the differences in light. The decks of ships were bright and sunny, but the holds were dim and dark. Smart pirates wore a patch over one eye to keep it adapted to the dark. When he went below deck, the pirate would switch the patch to the outdoor eye. The eye that had been wearing the patch would easily adjust to seeing in the dim light.

And yes, pirates did have parrots, just not usually as pets. In the 1700s, parrots were considered exotic pets and wealthy Europeans would pay great sums of money to own the brightly colored birds. Pirates liked money, so they captured as many of the tropical birds as possible and sold them for a hefty profit when they reached shore.

The First Pirates

Some of the first pirates robbed ships in the Greek Islands. In 500 BC, there were lots of cargo ships trading along the Mediterranean coast. Pirates attacked these ships and stole their cargo of copper, silver, and amber.

Pirate Practice

Bake Some Sea Biscuits

Pirate's Cooking Recipes

The sailors called them molar breakers and worm castles, but sea biscuits were a staple for every sailor in the 1600 and 1700s. They could be stored for months and still be eaten, but they would often get infested with weevils. The sailors had to brush off the bugs and eat the biscuits.

You can make your own sea biscuits, but leave out the bugs!

Materials:

- ❏ 4 parts flour
- ❏ 1 part water
- ❏ Salt to taste

Make dough by mixing the flour, water, and salt. Roll it out, about 1/2 inch thick, on a floured surface. Cut into square pieces about 2 1/2 to 3 inches. Place each cracker on a baking sheet, poke holes in the cracker with a fork, and bake at 250 degrees for one hour or until lightly browned.

Pirate Training
Shipwreck Salvage

Pirates often had to deal with being shipwrecked or stranded. When their ship broke apart, they had to make some quick decisions about what they would save. You can make and play your own shipwreck game.

Materials:

- ☐ 30 blank index cards
- ☐ Pens or markers
- ☐ A group of five or six friends

Before your friends arrive, make your shipwreck salvage cards. On each card, write an item that might be found in a pirate's wreck, such as gold, jewels, cannons, blankets, medicine, dried meat, silver, rope, etc. Include some useless things too, like fish bones and dead rats.

After you have made the cards, lay them face down at the finish line. Then divide your friends into two teams. This will run like a relay race. On "go," one pirate from each team will race to the finish line and pick up a salvage item.

The game is over when all of the cards are gone. But the winner is declared by which team has the most useful items. Fish bones and dead rats will not be useful, but ropes and a compass will. You can have fun discussing which items will be the most useful and which team should be the winner.

Team #1: Shipwreck Items	Team #2: Shipwreck Items

Weapons, Words, & Wardrobe

Dress Code

Imagine if the United States government made a law that only people who lived in Alabama could wear athletic shoes. Anyone who dared to wear athletic shoes in New York, California, Texas, or any other state had to pay a $50,000 fine. Imagine if this new law declared a dress code for everybody in the whole country. Only people in Montana could wear jeans. Only people in Kansas could wear T-shirts. And only the president and his family could wear the color purple.

That would be crazy and really wrong.

But that's exactly what happened in Elizabethan England when Queen Elizabeth declared the sumptuary laws. This was a dress code that was enforced throughout England. Only nobility were allowed to wear clothes that were purple, indigo blue, crimson, black, gold, or silver. A common person was only permitted to wear colors like grey, brown, beige, and green. They could wear blue but "not deep rich indigo blue but dyed with woad." (Woad was a common plant used for dye.)

The sumptuary laws also regulated the type of material from which clothes could be made. Nobility could wear silks, velvets, furs, and embroidered cloth. The regular folks could not. Then, there were rules about clothing that you *had* to wear. All of the common people had to wear a woolen cap on Sundays and holidays.

The purpose of the sumptuary laws was to keep a clear distinction between the classes. During the Middle Ages, common people could not afford to buy expensive cloth, furs, or special dyes. It was very easy to tell the nobility from the lower class people. But during the late 1500s and early 1600s, common people began to work as merchants, shop owners, and tradespeople. They earned enough money to be able to purchase cloth and goods that looked like the nobility. The dukes and duchesses were horrified. The sumptuary laws were passed to keep the common people in their place.

Pirates became heroes to people throughout England when they began wearing velvet coats stolen from rich nobles. It was seen as an act of defiance and a slap in the face for the snotty nobility. It was one of the reasons that pirates were cheered by everyday people.

Pirates were mainly common sailors, most of whom learned their trade in the navy. Their usual clothing would have wide puffy trousers made of canvas. The trousers were usually banded at the knee but some sailors cut off the band. This made the sailors' pants look like baggy shorts. These were practical for the work they needed to do. They also wore a simple grey or beige cloth shirt that could be tucked into their pants. They had woolen caps and short jackets.

Pirates wore the same type of clothing for their everyday work on the ship. But for special occasions or when they went ashore, they pulled out their fine stolen clothing. They went out to local pubs wearing richly embroidered coats and hats that were made for wealthy gentlemen. The pirates flaunted their red and indigo shirts and even wore the fine leather boots taken from rich gentlemen. It made their wealthy victims even angrier, but it made the common folks laugh.

There are numerous stories of pirate captains who dressed for battle. Both Blackbeard and Calico Jack were known to change out of their common seaman's clothing and put on their finest clothes before going into battle. It wasn't just that they were vain and wanted to look good in a fight. The fine clothing was a statement of rebellion against the crown and the unfair rules imposed by the nobility.

It was also a warning to their victims. By wearing the fancy clothes, the pirate was sending the message that he and his crew had already been successful in stealing from other wealthy people. The pirate was not scared, but the rich passengers on the ship should be!

How Much Did Pirates Pay to Have Their Ears Pierced?*

Pirates pieced their ears and wore gold earrings not because they were making a fashion statement but because they were superstitious. Pirates believed that piecing your ear would improve or even cure bad eyesight. Some believed that pierced ears helped prevent seasickness. And other people believed that wearing an earring could protect a man from drowning. None of these stories were true.

There was one benefit to wearing hoop earrings. The pirates who fired the ship's cannons dangled wads of wax from their earrings to use as earplugs.

*A buccaneer, of course! Get it? A buck an ear.

Pirate Attack!

Sailing has always been dangerous. Storms can destroy a ship or blow it off course. Rocks can crack the hull and sink the boat. But the worst disaster for any sea captain was an attack by pirates.

The crew was always on the lookout for other ships. A sailor with a spyglass or small telescope would search the horizon for white sails. Once a ship was spotted, the crew tried to see what flag it was flying. If it was the flag of their own country or a country that was a friend, the captain would not feel threatened. But if it was the flag of an enemy country, the crew knew it could be attacked by privateers who would raid the ship and steal their cargo.

Pirates often kept several sets of flags on their vessel to try to fool the other ships. It was called flying under false colors. The captain of the ship would allow the pirates to come close to them, thinking they were friendly and wanting to exchange news or goods. But when they got close, the pirates would attack.

The pirates dropped dinghies, or smaller boats, into the water and rowed up to the side of the ship. First they would break or disable the rudder of the target ship so there could be no escape. Then they threw grappling hooks and rope onto the deck and climbed up the sides of the ship. They came armed with cutlasses, multiple pistols, axes, and tomahawks.

The first person they attacked was the sailor at the ship's wheel. Sometimes there was a terrible battle, with both ships shooting cannons and sailors shooting and stabbing each other until one side was decimated. Pirates had reputations of being ruthless and of killing everyone on the ship. Sometimes they would take everyone who had survived and maroon them on an island without supplies. Other times they sold people as slaves or held them for ransom. Nobody wanted to be attacked by pirates.

But fighting was not always in the best interest of the pirates. Their whole goal was to take the cargo. If they could get the sailors to give up the cargo without a fight, it meant there was no damage to their payload. For that reason some pirates began flying their own flags, called "Jolly Rogers." They would hoist their own flag when they came close to the other ship. Sailors knew the flags of each pirate and their reputation for ruthlessness. Often the crew would bargain with the pirates to spare their lives if they gave up the cargo without a fight. This was a great deal for the pirates, but not such a great deal for the people trying to sell their goods and ship them to other countries. Many merchants lost shiploads of cargo to pirates.

The Flag Still Flies

A pirate flag is still flown by English submarines when they are returning to their base. This tradition started in World War I when a submarine's crew raised the pirate flag after they successfully completed a mission.

Most of the pirate flags were black with some form of skull and crossbones—a universal symbol for something that is dangerous. Pirates wanted to scare the other ships so they wouldn't fight. Therefore, they tried to make their flags as frightening as possible, with each pirate flying his own style of flag.

The famous pirate Blackbeard flew a flag with a black background and white horned skeleton holding an hourglass and spearing a heart. It was his way of telling other ships that he would gladly kill them if they resisted. Calico Jack's flag had a skull over two crossed cutlasses and Edward Low flew a black flag with a red skeleton. No matter what the flag looked like, it was a warning that every sailor understood: Be ready to surrender your cargo and possibly your lives.

THE JOLLY ROGERS

Here are some of the Jolly Rogers flown by real pirates.

Christopher Moody

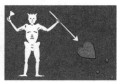

Blackbeard

Calico Jack

Henry Avery (Every)

Thomas Tew

Edward Low

Emmanuel Wynne

Stede Bonnet

Bartholomew Roberts

Fast and Furious

Fighting was the main job of a pirate. If he could be tough in battle and knew how to work on a ship, he was going to be a successful pirate. The tools of a pirate were the same tools of any sailor or navy man. He needed a ship, weapons, and the ability to swing an axe and shoot a gun.

Pirates preferred their ships to be lean and fast. Many people think that pirates wanted to capture and sail huge 40-gun warships, but that just isn't true. Pirates liked to be able to travel fast so they could get in and out quickly. They used smaller sloops that were not weighed down by heavy armaments.

Two of the pirate's favorite ships were the sloop and the schooner. These ships were both fast and had a shallow draft. This allowed pirates to hide in shallow coastal waters where large warships would be grounded. A single-masted sloop was one of the fastest ships of the time. It could hold 75 pirates and 10 cannons. That was enough men and weapons to be able to attack a large vessel, but it was still light and fast enough to get away quickly.

Cannons were a must on a pirate ship, but they were not usually used to try to sink the ship. Pirates wanted to disable their victims' craft so they could board and ransack it. Because they weren't trying to down the ship, they used ammunition that would take out riggings and sails. Instead of 8-pound cannon balls, they used smaller round shot. This was a group of small loose-fitting balls that could travel farther than heavy shot. They were effective at tearing through sails. Bar and chain shot was another favorite ammunition. This consisted of two halves of a cannon ball attached together with a bar or chain. These shots would wrap around masts and rip them to shreds, thus disabling the ship.

Grappling hooks, or boarding hooks, were used by pirates to catch the rigging of an enemy ship. The hooks were attached to a length of rope and thrown onto the other ship. When they caught the rigging, the pirates would pull the other ship close so they could jump on board.

Before they boarded the victim's ship, pirates would sometimes throw caltrops on the deck. Caltrops were a small piece of iron with four sharp points. Because most sailors worked barefoot, the caltrops were a nasty weapon. When a sailor would step on the caltrop, he would receive deep puncture wounds in his feet.

Once pirates boarded a ship, the fighting was fast and furious. They wanted to subdue the crew, take the cargo and get away as fast as possible. Most pirates carried several weapons so they could keep fighting even if one gun ran out of ammunition. If all of their guns were spent, they used knives and swords.

Flintlock pistols were a favorite weapon of pirates. They were fairly reliable in their firing mechanism and more accurate than a musket or blunderbuss. They fired a single shot and then had to be reloaded. Because of this, pirates often carried more than one pistol. Another problem with firearms was that during this time period, if the gunpowder got wet, the weapon would not fire accurately.

Pirates almost always kept a cutlass at their side. This is a knife with a blade about 2 feet long. It was made of thick metal and had a single edge. It was strong and sturdy enough to chop through heavy ropes, canvas, or even flesh and bone.

Grenades were also an essential pirate weapon. These were hollow balls of glass or metal that were filled with gunpowder and lit with a fuse. They worked as a small bomb, blowing holes in ships and people wherever they landed. Sometimes the pirates would fill the balls with a chemical substance that smelled horrendous and set them off on their enemies. These were called stinkpots. The chemicals would cause the sailors to vomit and pass out.

But the greatest weapon a pirate had was the information he could gather. Pirates tried to learn as much information as they could about incoming and outgoing ships. They interrogated sailors and passengers on the vessels they captured. If they thought it would give them information about wealthy merchant vessels, then they would torture their prisoners to learn about shipping schedules and cargo. By learning when, where, and what merchants were shipping, pirates were able to use the element of surprise as a weapon—the best weapon a smart pirate could have.

Arrr! Pirate Talk

What did real pirates sound like? Did they actually shout things like "Shiver me timbers!" and "Blow the man down"? And why do pirates always say "Arrr"?

The truth is, there is not much scientific evidence about how pirates talked. Audio recording devices had not been invented in the 1600s and 1700s, so no one alive today has heard historical pirates speak. And there is very little written record of pirate language, because most of the pirates could not read or write. There are a few documents written by literate pirates. In these letters, the pirates used the same words and terminology as other sailors of their time.

The popular idea of how pirates talked comes from Hollywood movies. Actor Lionel Barrymore played a pirate in a movie during the 1930s. He seems to be the actor who first used the "Arrr" sound associated with pirates. In the 1950s, there was a very popular movie made based on the famous book *Treasure Island*. The actor who played the role of Long John Silver was Robert Newton. He also used the "Arrr" sound and added famous phrases like "Shiver me timbers" and "Blow the man down."

In reality, pirates probably talked the same way that other sailors did. Their vocabulary would be different from people who worked on land because they spoke the slang of sailors. Pirates were from many different countries and spoke a variety of languages. They did learn common nautical terms so they could communicate. They would also have used slang phrases that were common during that time period.

These are just some of the words that sailors and pirates of the 1600 and 1700s would likely have used.

Pirate Talk	Translation
ahoy	hello
avast	stop and give attention
aye	yes, I agree
bail out	(1) remove water from a swamped boat; (2) help a friend get out of trouble
belay	(1) sailing term meaning to fasten a rope around a pin to secure the running gear; (2) a command to stop
bilge	(1) lowest part inside the ship and the first place to show signs of leakage—considered the filthiest part of the ship; (2) nonsense and foolish talk
bilge rat	(1) a rat living in the bilge of the ship; (2) an insulting name
board	to get on or in a ship
booty	plunder or loot from a battle

Pirate Talk	Translation
bow	forward part of the ship
chew the fat	(1) eating a portion of sailor's daily ration of tough salt-cured pork; (2) friendly conversation
crossing the line	(1) ceremony performed when sailor crossed the equator for the first time; (2) going too far
Davy Jones's locker	the bottom of the sea
deadlights	eyes
ditty bag	bag where a sailor kept his valuables
dog	a mild insult
fair winds	goodbye and good luck
flogging	punishment by whipping
grog	rum diluted with water and sometimes lemon juice
grub	food
hands	the sailors on a ship, the crew
hornpipe	single-reeded musical instrument that sailors played
jury rig	a temporary repair to keep a disabled ship sailing
keelhauling	severe punishment where a sailor was dragged under the bottom of the boat from one side to another
lubber	someone who does not go to sea
lights	lungs
lookout	sailor posted to keep watch on the horizon for land or signs of other ships

Pirate Talk	Translation
mayday	distress signal that came from the French "m'aidez," meaning "help me"
no quarter	surrender will not be accepted
pillage	to raid, rob, and attack a target on the shore
port	the left side of the ship
run a shot across the bow	warning shot to another ship's captain
scuttle	to sink a ship on purpose
scuttlebutt	gossip and rumors
seadog	old pirate or sailor
smartly	to do something quickly
spyglass	a telescope
starboard	the right side of the ship
stern	the back part of the ship
swag	loot

Long John Silver Has Something to Say

You can listen to actor Robert Newton as he plays the role of Long John Silver. Check it out at https://www.youtube.com/watch?v=I2asCBs8Yrw&feature=related

Build a Better Boat

Pirates wanted to be able to carry as much treasure as they could possibly could. You can experiment with building a tinfoil boat and loading it up with the most cargo you can.

Materials:

- ❑ Tinfoil
- ❑ Bowl
- ❑ Scissors
- ❑ Pennies
- ❑ Water

Sample boat shape

Cut a piece of tinfoil 5 x 6 inches. Fold the aluminum into the shape of a boat.

Place the boat in the bowl of water. Begin adding pennies for the boat's cargo.

See how many pennies your boat can carry before it sinks.

Experiment with making the boat into a different shape and see if you can load it with more pennies. What shape holds the most pennies?

Pirate Training

Jolly Roger

Every self-respecting pirate should have his or her own Jolly Roger. You can create your own design and raise the flag over your pirate's cabin (your bedroom).

Materials:

- ❏ Black construction paper
- ❏ White crayons
- ❏ Scissors

Use the following page to sketch out your design ideas. Next, cut the construction paper into the shape of a flag. You can make it a rectangular or triangular shape.

Decide what symbols you want to use to tell the world about yourself. Are you a fearsome pirate with a sword? Do you want to scare people with a skeleton?

Once you have designed and colored your Jolly Roger, hoist it up in your home and warn the world that a pirate lives in your home!

My Jolly Roger

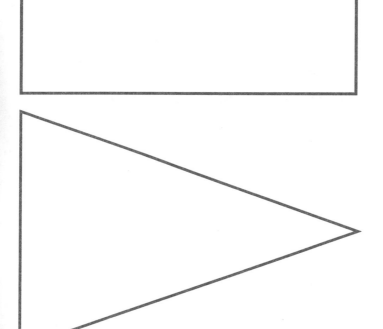

Images I chose for my Jolly Roger:_____

_____

What does this say about me as a pirate? _____

_____

VIPs

Very Important Pirates

Cheng I Sao

She was the most powerful pirate to ever sail the seas. She had 50,000 sailors who worked for her and commanded more than 600 ships. In 1810, Cheng I Sao was the terror of the Chinese government.

At a time when American women didn't have the right to vote and many women could not even own property, Cheng I Sao was a feared leader obeyed by thousands of men. She ran her pirates like they were a military operation. Instead of waiting for unsuspecting victims to sail over the horizon, Cheng I Sao planned who and where her pirates would attack. She knew the shipping lines and the trade routes that other countries used. She sent her ships to attack during trading season.

Cheng I Sao also set up warehouses inland to store the plunder they stole and contracted with farmers and merchants to keep her pirates supplied with food, tools, and weapons.

Cheng I Sao was not always a pirate; her name means "widow of Zheng" and she did not become famous until she married the sea robber, Zheng Yi. It is said that she would only consent to marry Zheng Yi if he agreed to make her his partner and give her half of his plunder. Zheng Yi must have agreed, because after they were married Cheng I Sao began helping run the Red Flag Fleet pirates.

For the next 6 years, they worked together as a team, raiding ships and stealing supplies, money, and valuables. With Cheng I Sao's help, the pirate fleet grew from 200 simple Chinese junks to an army of vessels that included ships and weapons from many different countries. But in November of 1807, disaster struck when Zheng Yi was caught in a typhoon and went down with his ship.

Cheng I Sao was determined to keep their empire alive, so she started working with other pirate groups to make a pirate-run government that was stronger than the official Chinese government. She had male and female pirates, children, farmers, and spies all working for her on land and sea. She provided a good living for the people who worked for her and in return she expected absolute obedience.

> Rules were simple. If people stole from the warehouse, they got their heads cut off. If people disobeyed an order, they got their heads cut off.

Rules were simple. If people stole from the warehouse, they got their heads cut off. If people disobeyed an order, they got their heads cut off. If a sailor took leave without permission, he got his head cut off. Not many people were willing to disagree with Cheng I Sao, not even many armies.

Several towns were tired of being raided by her pirates, though, so they banded together to form an army to fight the Red Flag Fleet. It didn't go well for the townspeople. Cheng I Sao's Red Flag Fleet destroyed the village's army and then cut the heads off all of the men.

Complaints about Cheng I Sao and her pirates reached the ears of the Chinese Emperor, and he decided to take matters into his own hands. He sent a huge fleet of ships to fight the Red Flag Fleet. The Emperor was sure that his navy could outfight the untrained pirates. He was wrong.

Cheng I Sao wasn't scared of the Emperor's armada. She sailed out with her fleet to meet the navy and defeated them easily. She also captured 63 of the Emperor's ships and convinced most of the surviving sailors to leave the navy and join her pirates. Of course, their choice was to either become a pirate or have their feet nailed to the deck of a ship. Most of them thought becoming a pirate was a good idea.

Left with a very small navy, the Emperor had to call upon the British and Portuguese Navies for help. The two super power navies banded together and fought a war against Cheng I Sao and her pirates for 2 years. Cheng I Sao won battle after battle.

Finally, the Chinese Emperor decided to try something different. If he couldn't beat the pirates, then he would offer them amnesty. If Cheng I Sao and her pirates would stop attacking the navy and return their plunder, the emperor would agree not to execute them. Cheng I Sao saw no advantage to this and dismissed the idea of amnesty.

But in a few months, Cheng I Sao surprised the Chinese government and

> Finally, the Chinese Emperor decided to try something different. If he couldn't beat the pirates, then he would offer them amnesty.

Grace O'Malley, Pirate Queen

When Grace O'Malley was young girl she wanted to be a sailor like her father and brothers. But in the 1540s, proper young ladies did not work as sailors. Grace horrified her mother by cutting off her long red hair and dressing as a boy. Grace's father gave in, and Grace spent the rest of her life at sea. She became a fearless leader and pirate who raided and robbed ships along the Gaelic coast. She never retired and was still an honored chieftain when she died at age 70.

showed up at the home of the Governor General of Canton. She offered a peace treaty that was on her terms.

Her terms included that out of her 50,000 pirate sailors, all but 376 of them would receive full amnesty. There was to be no punishment at all for their crimes. They were also to be allowed to keep all of their plunder. In addition, any of her men who wanted to were allowed to join the military. Cheng I Sao's new husband was given 20 ships to command in the Chinese Navy. And Cheng I Sao was allowed to keep her entire fortune, plus she asked to be given the noble title of "Lady by Imperial Decree." The governor decided it was an offer he couldn't refuse.

Cheng I Sao was 35 years old when she retired from pirating. She lived in Canton for the rest of her life and died at the age of 69. She was both a mother and grandmother, and her children probably thought twice before they disobeyed.

The Lioness of Brittany

Jeanne de Clisson was angry. The French had wrongfully beheaded her husband and she wanted revenge. In 1343, the noblewoman teamed up with the king of England. With his help, she purchased three ships, painted them all black, and dyed their sails red. Jeanne's Black Fleet patrolled the English Channel, hunting down French ships, attacking them, and killing the crews. She would leave one or two witnesses alive so they could report the news to the French king.

The Real Blackbeard

A band of pirates swarmed over the ship. They threw grappling hooks onto the deck and scrambled up the ropes, carrying knives in their teeth. Waves of men climbed up the ropes and onto the ship until the pirates nearly outnumbered the ship's crew. Then the pirate leader boarded the ship. He was a tall man with a wild mane of black hair and a beard that had smoke and sparks flying out of it. He carried two swords and had a sash of guns and cutlasses strapped to his body. With his blood-red coat and fiery beard, he looked like a devil come straight out of Hades.

The crew knew they had just been attacked by none other than the famous pirate Blackbeard. They were terrified and gave up without firing a single weapon. Blackbeard was happy; everything had gone according to his plan.

Edward Teach was the man known as Blackbeard, and from 1716 to 1718, he was the most feared pirate to sail the seas. But despite his frightening appearance and his evil reputation, Blackbeard was not a bloodthirsty pirate. There is no evidence that Blackbeard ever killed anyone who was not trying to kill him. Instead of killing and maiming his victims as some pirates did, Blackbeard preferred to scare them into submission.

He grew his beard long, and when he was going into battle, he would weave wicks laced with gunpowder through his beard and set them on fire. The slow-burning wicks caused his face to be shrouded in smoke and sparks. Superstitious sailors were sure he was the devil incarnate and were happy to give Blackbeard what he wanted if he would leave them alone.

Once the crew had surrendered, Blackbeard ordered his men to search the ship and take everything of value. The pirates would load up all of the valuables, taking everything

from money, weapons, and wine and rum casks, to passenger's fancy clothing and the ship's navigational tools.

Once Blackbeard was sure that he had everything of value, he usually let the crew and passengers sail away unharmed. If he met with a crew that resisted, Blackbeard would fight. After he had won the battle and taken the ship's goods, he would punish the resisters by marooning them and burning the ship. It was far less cruel than many pirates who killed everyone on board.

Blackbeard's ship was named the *Queen Anne's Revenge*. He captured the ship while he was working for a pirate named Benjamin Hornigold and was rewarded with command of the 40-gun ship. Hornigold was Blackbeard's tutor in the skills of piracy and together they were a fearsome team. They were joined by another pirate, Stede Bonnet. He was not as fearsome, and with the urging of Bonnet's crew, Blackbeard took over the ship. Bonnet was held a prisoner, but was not killed or marooned. For several months, the captains and crews of the three ships sailed up and down the Atlantic coast of America terrorizing the ships in the area. They robbed merchant ships, taking clothes, guns, ammunition, food, and money. Then they would sell the goods at local ports for less money than the merchants charged. The locals liked the good deals that they were getting from Blackbeard and considered him their hero.

During 1717, the British government offered a pardon to any pirates who would submit to the king and promise to stop their pirating ways. Hornigold decided to take the pardon and retired from pirating. Blackbeard said "no": He was going to stay a pirate, so he set off for the Caribbean. During the next few months, Blackbeard and his crew captured an 80-ton trading ship named the *Adventure*. After that, he captured another ship in the Bay of Honduras and four smaller sloops. Soon Blackbeard had his own small navy of pirate ships. They spent the rest of 1718 attacking and robbing ships from Cuba all the way to South Carolina.

In May of 1718, Blackbeard decided he needed a promotion, so he declared himself to be a commodore rather than a mere pirate captain. Then he immediately ordered his ships and crew to blockade the port of Charleston. This meant that Blackbeard's pirates stopped every ship that was entering or leaving the port. Because the town had no guard ship, Blackbeard had successfully taken over one of the busiest ports in the southeast American colonies. News of Blackbeard's daring attack spread throughout the colonies and government officials were horrified. If one pirate crew could cause so much trouble, what would happen if the pirates banded together?

The British government decided they had to get rid of the pirates once and for all. They planned to hire sailors and pay them to become pirate hunters. One of those sailors was Lieutenant Robert Maynard and his specific mission was to hunt down and destroy the notorious pirate Blackbeard.

Maynard set off with two sloops and 70 men. On November 21, he tracked down Blackbeard and his crew onboard the small ship, *Adventure*. Blackbeard and a small number of pirates were resting along the shore of Ocracoke Island enjoying an evening of entertainment. Lieutenant Maynard's spy reported that Blackbeard appeared to have no more than 25 sailors with him.

Maynard waited until daybreak and then ordered his ships to attack Blackbeard and the *Adventure*. The crew of the *Adventure* spotted Maynard's ships right away and hoisted their sails and maneuvered to point her guns at Maynard's ships. Maynard told his

Blackbeard's Ship Found!

Nearly 300 years after Blackbeard's death, marine archaeologists have discovered the remains of Blackbeard's flagship, the *Queen Anne's Revenge*. Buried in water and sand off the coast of North Carolina, divers have found the 3,000 pound anchor that Blackbeard and his crew used. They also found cannons, improvised missiles, and doctor's tools. What they haven't found is any treasure. It is believed that Blackbeard emptied the ship of loot and then wrecked the *Queen Anne* on purpose so he wouldn't have to share his booty with all of his crew.

crew to keep sailing toward the pirates. Blackbeard ordered his men to fire their guns and the blast rocked the first ship and killed or wounded nearly a third of the men.

Maynard still had another ship and he had told his men to hide in the hold. Blackbeard's men observed that there was only a small crew on board Maynard's ship and as they sailed close, the pirates jumped aboard Maynard's ship and began to fight. It was then that Maynard gave the call to his men hidden below deck to come out and fight.

Blackbeard's men were surprised by the attack. Screams and the sound of gunfire filled the air. Blackbeard and his men were outnumbered, but they fought with all of their might. Maynard and Blackbeard came face to face and fired their flintlocks at each other. Blackbeard drew his cutlass. Maynard drew his sword. Blackbeard broke Maynard's sword in half. Blackbeard rushed in to attack Maynard, but Blackbeard was slashed across the throat by one of Maynard's men.

Blackbeard was badly wounded, but he kept fighting—attacking and killing his enemies until he collapsed and died. When they saw their leader was dead, Blackbeard's men surrendered. After the end of the battle, Maynard examined Blackbeard's body and reported that he had been shot at least five times and had 20 knife cuts. Maynard's crew cut Blackbeard's head off and suspended it from the bow of Maynard's sloop. They threw his body into the ocean.

The remainder of Blackbeard's crew was captured and hanged for their crimes as pirates. It was the end of the reign of Blackbeard, but his story lives on in history as being one of the mightiest pirates ever to sail the seas.

Black Bart

Captain Bartholomew Roberts with two ships, the *Royal Fortune* and *Ranger*, takes sail off the Cost of Guiney, 1721

John Roberts' feet were tough and calloused from running barefoot across the rough wooden ship deck and scrambling up the ropes and riggings. He was only 13 years old, but he was already an experienced cabin boy. He spent his days helping the cook prepare meals, cleaning the captain's cabin, and running errands for all of the older sailors on the ship.

He liked life onboard a ship and quickly learned all of the different jobs a sailor needed to know. He enjoyed working with the ship's riggings, checking the hull for leaks, and helping with repairs. He learned how to read the tides and stars. He understood the winds and weather and knew what to do in case of a storm. Sailing was the only career he ever wanted. His world would have been perfect if he could just be the captain of his own ship.

But John Roberts was born in 1682, and during that time, a common Welsh man would never be promoted to captain, no matter how smart he was. A captain had to be wealthy enough to purchase a share in the ship. Most captains were sons of wealthy merchants. Roberts served under many different captains, and often knew that the captain was not nearly as smart or capable as he was. It was enough to make any man angry and resentful.

By 1719, Roberts was serving as a third mate on a slave ship named *Princess*. They were shipping slaves from the Gold Coast of Africa to the Americas. That summer, Roberts's life changed.

One day in June, two pirate ships were sighted by the crew of the *Princess*. The two vessels bore down on the *Princess* and before they could even start to escape, the *Princess* was invaded. The fight was short and the *Princess* was taken over by pirate captain Howell Davis. Some of the captured slaves volunteered to join the pirate crew. And the pirate crew decided to take some of the best sailors on the *Princess* and force them to work for the pirates. Roberts was one of the sailors taken.

At first, Roberts was unhappy with his new job as a pirate, but Captain Davis was a fellow Welshman and he took a liking to Roberts. Captain Davis soon learned that Roberts was a talented navigator and began consulting him about where to go and whom to attack. He liked being able to talk to Roberts in Welsh so nobody else could understand them.

At last, Roberts had found a ship and a captain who knew his worth. But just a few weeks later, Captain Davis and his landing party were attacked and killed on Principe Island. The pirates elected Roberts to be the new captain of the crew. Roberts may not have wanted to be a pirate, but he decided that if he was going to be a pirate, he might as well be the captain. He accepted.

His first act was to get revenge for the death of his friend Captain Davis. He led the crew back to the island of Principe and attacked the fort and village. They killed a large number of the men of the island and stole all they could carry back to the ships. It was the start of Roberts' short and violent career.

At this time, Roberts changed his first name to Bartholomew, probably to try to disguise his real identity. Many pirates took an alias or used different names. Bartholomew Roberts became known as one of the most dangerous pirates in the world and was sometimes referred to as Black Bart because of his evil ways. Once Roberts decided to be a pirate, he did it with gusto. He is remembered for saying "a merry life and a short one shall be my motto."

Within a few days of the attack on Principe, Roberts led his pirates to capture a Dutch slave ship and a British ship called the *Experiment*. From there, the crew voted to sail to Brazil. For the next 2 1/2 years, Roberts and his pirates captured an astounding 470 ships.

With his success, Roberts began to embrace his pirate life. He started wearing fine silk and velvet coats and a fancy captain's hat. He carried a sword in his hand and kept two pistols slung over his shoulders. The clothes were, of course, all stolen from victims of his raids.

He ruled his pirate crew with a strict set of rules—a pirate code. There were not to be any women allowed on the ship, and if anyone was caught carrying a woman to sea in disguise, the punishment was death. It was the same punishment for deserting the ship in time of battle. If any pirate robbed another pirate, he would have his nose and ears slit and be put ashore. If a pirate stole from the company, he would be marooned. But every pirate was to have an equal vote in affairs of the moment. This included which ships to attack and where they were going to sail.

By the beginning of 1722, the British were fed up with Roberts and the damage he was doing to their ships and trade. The Royal Navy was on the hunt for Roberts and his pirate crew. On February 5, the *HMS Swallow* found Roberts and three of his ships resting in Cape Lopez on the west coast of Africa.

The commander of the *Swallow* veered away as she came in sight of the pirate ships, making the pirates think the *Swallow* was trying to run.

The *Ranger* and its captain, James Skyrme, gave chase while the other pirate ships remained anchored. Once the *Swallow* had led the *Ranger* out of earshot, the Royal Navy opened the gun ports and fired on the pirate ship. Ten pirates were killed and Skyrme had his leg shot off by a cannonball, but he refused to leave the deck. The fight was bloody and furious, but in the end the Royal Navy captured the pirates and their ship.

Five days later the *Swallow* sailed back to where Roberts and the rest of the pirates were anchored. Roberts and his crew had just captured another ship the day before and the men had spent the night celebrating. When the *Swallow* sailed into view, most of Roberts's crew were too drunk to even try to fight. The *Swallow* fired its guns and Captain Bartholomew Roberts was killed.

His men knew that Roberts wanted to be buried at sea so that the navy would not make an example of him by displaying his

Roberts' first flag shows himself and Death holding an hourglass

body with chains and threw him overboard.

The battle continued for 2 more hours, but the pirates were outgunned and were finally captured. Out of the 272 pirates who were arrested, 65 were sold into slavery. The other men were tried for piracy and 54 of them were hanged. The rest of the men were either acquitted or forced to sign indentured servant contracts with the Royal African Company.

The death of Bartholomew Roberts marked the end of the golden age of piracy. Roberts had been a folk legend to many people. The poor felt like Roberts was a sort of Robin Hood, stealing from the rich and then selling his goods to the poor

for less money that the wealthy ship merchants charges them. Even though he killed disobedient crewmen and murdered innocent people in raids, the people still saw him as a hero and mourned his death.

ABH AMH

Black Bart's last flag showed him standing on two skulls, representing the heads of a Barbadian and a Martiniquian

Sadie the Goat

The businessman looked cautiously up and down the street, watching for carriages, horses, and any suspicious looking people. The streets of New York were a dangerous place in 1869, full of petty criminals waiting to ambush anyone with a little money. The man heaved a sigh of relief as he made it across the street. If he could just make it out of the Bloody Fourth Ward and back to a safer neighborhood!

Suddenly he saw a small person running toward him. Before the businessman knew what had happened, Sadie Farrell had head-butted him in the stomach. Stunned, the businessman doubled over. Then Sadie's partner aimed his slingshot and hit the man in the head with a rock. The businessman crumpled to the ground, unconscious. Sadie and her partner then proceeded to steal everything of value. They took his money, watch, and even stole his shirt, pants, and shoes. When the poor man regained conscious, he would learn that he had been robbed by the famous Sadie the Goat, a hoodlum who got her name by ramming her victims like a billy goat.

Sadie had grown up on the rough streets of New York's Fourth Ward, and by the time she was a teenager, she was an expert criminal. She was small, thin, and quite clever. She needed a male partner to be successful in her robberies, but Sadie was the one who made the plans. Sadie had a tough reputation and she needed it to stay alive in the Fourth Ward. But one day Sadie got in a fight with the wrong person. She took on Gallus Mag.

Mag was a huge woman who worked as a bouncer at a local bar. Gallus Mag was 6 feet tall and could easily toss a grown man out of the bar. She also had a talent for biting off people's ears. She would put the person in a headlock and then chomp down. After she bit off the ear, she would throw the person out of the bar. The ear however, stayed with Mag. She pickled all of the ears she collected and kept them in jars behind the bar.

Sadie didn't fare any better in her fight with Gallus Mag than anyone else. Mag bit her ear off and threw Sadie out of the bar. Sadie the Goat had one less ear and was a disgrace as a hoodlum. Sadie left the Fourth Ward in embarrassment and tried to start up work as a thief on the West Side docks. But when she saw the members of a gang try to steal a ship, Sadie had a better idea. Why not become a pirate?

Sadie managed to convince some of the members of the Charlton Street Gang that with her as their leader, they could be the best pirates on the Hudson River. With instructions from Sadie, the men managed to steal a small sloop that was anchored in the river. Sadie quickly hoisted a Jolly Roger flag and set her crew to robbing and plundering the farms and mansions up and down the Hudson River.

From spring through summer, Sadie and her crew managed to acquire a substantial amount of loot. They would hide it in coves of the river and then sell it to make cash. But by the end of the summer, the good farmers and townspeople had enough of the pirates and banded together to ambush the Charleston Gang as they came ashore. Many of them were captured, and Sadie found herself without a pirate crew.

Sadie gave up her work as a pirate and returned to the Fourth Ward, but now she had the title of "Queen of the Waterfront." The other thugs and thieves could respect a woman who had been a pirate. Sadie even felt safe enough to make up with Gallus Mag. Mag graciously returned Sadie's pickled ear to her. Sadie used the cash she earned from her pirating days to open up her own gin mill. She also purchased a locket and placed her severed ear inside. She wore the locket around her neck for the rest of her life.

Sadie Farrell gave up her work as a pirate and returned to the Fourth Ward, but now she had the title of "Queen of the Waterfront"

Really Rotten Pirate

The gentleman's three-piece suit, circa 1700

Stede Bonnet was a really rotten pirate. He didn't know how to sail a ship, he wasn't good at fighting, and he didn't like to be dirty. He was such a terrible pirate that his entire crew asked Blackbeard to take over their ship.

Bonnet was not a typical pirate. He grew up in a wealthy family on the island of Barbados. As an adult, he served in the British Army and retired with the rank of major and went home to run his large plantation. Most pirates were people who could not find another way to make a living. They were escaped slaves, disgruntled sailors, or seamen who were angry with their government. Bonnet was none of these.

He had only been on a ship as a passenger and had never spent much time at sea. He was wealthy, privileged, and seemed to have no quarrel with the British government. Plus

Stede Bonnet

he had a wife and children, but none of that seemed to matter to Bonnet. He decided one day in 1717 that he was going to be a pirate. He very responsibly made legal arrangements for his wife and a business partner to manage his plantation and investments. He told them that he would be leaving Barbados, but he didn't tell them what he had planned.

The next thing he did was to buy a sloop and outfit it with 10 guns. This was not the way most pirates went into business. They stole and pillaged to get their boats, but Bonnet had money, so he bought his ship and named it *Revenge*. Then he began recruiting a pirate crew.

The sailors and pirates that he hired knew that their captain was a little different from other leaders they had sailed with in the past. Bonnet didn't dress in sailor's canvas pants. He wore gentlemen's knee breeches, fine shirts, and even sported a periwig (a men's wig that was fashionable during the 1700s).

His clothes, his wealthy background, and his love of books and reading earned him the nickname of "The Gentleman Pirate." But Bonnet was anything but gentlemanly when it came to his crew and the people he attacked. Bonnet abused his crew and killed his prisoners. He wanted to be feared as a pirate, and he believed in being harsh and cruel.

During the first few months of Bonnet's piracy, he managed to plunder several vessels along the coast of Virginia and the Carolinas. But it was really because of the expertise of his experienced pirate crew that he had any success. Bonnet himself was inept at sailing and had no real idea of how to manage sailors.

When Bonnet sighted another pirate ship off the coast of the Carolinas, he was thrilled to find that the captain was none other than the famous pirate, Blackbeard. Bonnet was excited to meet Blackbeard, and so was his crew. As a matter of fact, the crew asked Blackbeard to please take over the ship and save them from the awful leadership of Bonnet.

Blackbeard obliged, but was amazingly kind in his dealings with Bonnet. He suggested to Bonnet that he would be much more comfortable in the quarters on Blackbeard's vessel where he could spend more of his time reading and studying instead of having to manage the rowdy crew of sailors.

Bonnet spent the next few months roaming Blackbeard's ship in his dressing gown, enjoying reading and tending to his collection of books. During this time, Blackbeard and Bonnet's crew held the harbor of Charleston under siege. They robbed every vessel that tried to enter or leave the port and kidnapped several prominent citizens. Blackbeard and the crews finally left after they were paid a ransom and given a chest of medical supplies.

After the siege was over, Blackbeard told Bonnet that he was going to go to the officials and seek a pardon for his pirating. At that time, the British government was offering pardons to pirates because they hoped that if they pardoned the pirates and made them promise to stop attacking their ships, the pirates would then settle down to live peaceful lives. Blackbeard convinced Bonnet that he should go to the government and ask for a pardon, too. He promised Bonnet that after they both received their pardons, they could divide the

Traditional depiction of Stede Bonnet's flag

plunder among all of their crew and Bonnet could sail off with his ship and Blackbeard would sail off in his own. The plan suited Bonnet, because he had figured out that he probably wasn't the best pirate on the seas, so Bonnet left his ship and went to get a pardon.

When Bonnet returned, he did find his ship, but all of the treasure and plunder was gone and so was Blackbeard and the rest of the crew. Bonnet had been tricked. Furious, Bonnet reorganized with a new crew and set out to seek revenge on Blackbeard.

Bonnet had learned a few things from his time with Blackbeard. He managed to assault and plunder a few more ships as he was looking for Blackbeard. He threatened civilians and captured prisoners. He tried to get paid ransom for his captives, but had very little success. In anger and frustration, he began killing and torturing the sailors on the ships he captured. He was always looking for information about Blackbeard, but Bonnet never found him. Instead pirate hunter Colonel William Rhett found Bonnet.

There was a fierce battle between the two ships. Bonnet declared he would blow himself up and his ship before he would ever surrender. But, as in the past, Bonnet's crew didn't follow their captain. Instead they gave up the ship, and Bonnet was captured with his men.

During the trial, Bonnet begged for forgiveness and mercy from the court and tried to blame everything on Blackbeard. It didn't work. Bonnet and 30 of his crew were convicted of piracy and hanged. It was a rotten end for a really rotten pirate.

The Legend of the Black Caesars

Many stories are told about the pirate Black Caesar; the question is who was the real Black Caesar and which stories are true?

One legend says Black Caesar was a tall African chief who met a sailing crew along the coast of the African continent in the late 1690s. Black Caesar and some of his tribesmen were lured onto the ship by the captain with promises of a feast of foreign foods. While Caesar and his men were on the ship, they were shown exotic animal furs, beautiful silks, and even a gold watch. These were amazing sights that the Africans had never seen. The men were so engrossed in the meal, the strange and different music, and the treasures that they did not realize that the ship was setting sail.

When Caesar and his tribesmen realized they had been tricked, they fought the sailors, but were overpowered and locked in chains—captured to be sold as slaves.

Chained in the damp dark hull of the ship, Caesar refused to eat. This was not what the captain wanted. He wanted to be able to sell the strong, healthy chief for a good price. One of the sailors eventually was able to become friends with Caesar and convinced him to eat.

When the slave ship reached the coast of Florida, it was caught in a huge storm and wrecked on the Florida reefs. As the ship lay floundering on the reef, the sailor who had befriended Caesar freed him from his chains. Caesar and the sailor then stole a long-boat, filled it with supplies and ammunition, and sailed to an island in the Florida Keys.

There Caesar and the sailor started their careers as pirates. They used the longboat as a lure to passing ships. They would pretend to be marooned sailors and when the ship would try to rescue them, Caesar and the sailor would attack and take control of the ship.

They were building a small pirate army with men and ships who knew the ins and outs of the Florida Keys. They were able to attack and then hide where other ships could not find them. All was going well until the sailor brought back a beautiful woman from one of the raids.

It is said that Caesar fell in love with the woman and was so terribly jealous that he fought a duel with his former friend and killed him. Caesar went on pirating and eventually joined forces with the pirate Blackbeard.

Caesar was with Blackbeard when Royal Navy Lieutenant Robert Maynard attacked Blackbeard and his pirate crew in 1718. Caesar stood in the gunpowder room with a lit torch. If the Royal Navy overpowered the pirate fleet, it was Caesar's job to blow up the ship so that the pirates would not be taken alive.

But in the fighting, Caesar was discovered and overpowered. He never got a chance to set off the explosives. Caesar was tried with the other pirates and hanged in Williamsburg, VA.

But that is just one story of Black Caesar—there is another, also about a pirate named Black Caesar. This man was a pirate for nearly 30 years in the early 1800s and operated along the coast of Florida by Sanibel and Captiva Islands. Florida's Black Caesar was born a slave on a French plantation in Haiti and was named Henri Caesar. He worked in the plantation lumberyard and suffered abuse by the hands of his foreman. When the slaves rebelled in Haiti, Henri joined the revolution. His first act was to kill the foreman.

Henri fought with the revolution until Haiti gained its independence from France in 1804. Then he decided to try his luck as a pirate. He managed to capture a Spanish ship in 1805 and set himself up with a pirate crew.

For more than 20 years, Henri attacked and raided small villages and lone ships near the islands of Cuba and the Bahamas. It was a very long career for a pirate. Most pirates only survived for 2 or 3 years. To survive as a pirate for more than 20 years was highly unusual.

Sometime in 1830, Henri Caesar disappeared. There is no record of what happened to him. Some say he was captured and burned to death as revenge for his pirating ways. Others believe that Henri fled the area when he learned that, in 1828, President Andrew Jackson had ordered an expedition to capture and kill all the pirates along the Florida coast. There is no record that Henri was among the pirates who were hanged. It is still a mystery what happened to him.

So which story is true? Maybe both or maybe neither. There are not any written historical records about the births, deaths, or trials of either of the pirates called Black Caesar, but that is true for many people of the time. What is known is that there were numerous Black men who served as pirates. The rosters of some of the famous pirate captains of the time show that a significant percentage of their crews were escaped slaves.

For example, Samuel Bellamy had 27 Black pirates on his crew, Edward England listed around 50 escaped slaves on his crew, Blackbeard had 60 Black pirates on board, and half of Olivier Levasseur's crew was made up of escaped slaves.

During a time when Africans were hunted, captured, and sold into slavery, piracy was seen as a place for slave to rebel and escape. They were given equal share of the plunder from the pirate attacks and they were given an equal vote in decision making. Many considered it a better chance at freedom than they had anywhere in America. And most would rather die a free pirate than live as a slave.

One rule that was different for the Black pirates was what happened to them when they were caught. Some of them were hanged like their White counterparts, but many were sent back to their former owners or sold back into slavery. And not all pirate captains were equal opportunity employers. Some pirate captains raided slave ships and stole the slaves simply to sell them.

The truth of the pirates known as Black Caesar may never be fully known. But their legends will go on through history.

The Successful Pirate

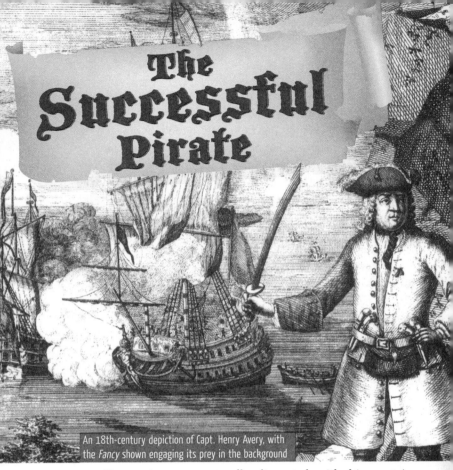

An 18th-century depiction of Capt. Henry Avery, with the *Fancy* shown engaging its prey in the background

Henry Avery was totally disgusted with his captain. Captain Gibson spent more of his time drinking rum than he did managing his ship, the *Charles II*. The crew hadn't been paid in months and as first mate, Avery had to hear all of the complaints from the other sailors.

Avery had been a seaman for a long time. He had served in the Royal Navy in the early 1690s and had only signed on as the first mate of the *Charles II* because he had been promised a share of the plunder the privateering ship was supposed to take. But it was looking like the whole adventure was going to be a disaster—all because of a drunken captain. Avery decided there was only one thing he could do. Lead a mutiny to take over the ship.

It wasn't hard for Avery to convince the other crewmen to join him. They were sick of Captain Gibson, too. And they wanted money—something they were definitely not getting with Gibson as captain. So they agreed to Avery's scheme.

It was a simple, but effective plan. The crew would simply wait until Captain Gibson was drunk and passed out in his cabin. Then Avery would lock him in and the crew would hoist anchor and set sail. By the time Gibson woke up out of his drunken stupor, they would be out at sea and Gibson would not be able to get help from the authorities.

Everything worked exactly as planned. With Gibson locked in his cabin and sleeping off his rum, the crew happily set sail. Hours later Captain Gibson rang the bell for his steward to come wait on him, but Henry Avery was the one who opened the door. Gibson demanded to know why the ship was at sea. Who had ordered this? What was going on?

Avery calmly explained that the crew had elected him as the new captain, and Gibson had two choices. He could become a member of the crew and serve under Avery, or he could get in one of the long boats and row himself back to shore. Gibson decided to take the offer of the boat and left thinking Avery was a generous man. Most crews would have killed the old captain and dumped his body at sea.

As newly elected captain, Avery called the crew together and told him about his plan for them to gain wealth and fame. He had heard stories about the rich Mughal Empire, whose ships sailed in the Indian Ocean. He thought that if they could capture one of these ships, then they would have gold, silks, and treasures beyond their wildest dreams. The crew heard the word "gold," and they happily signed on to be pirates and hunt down the ships. They changed the name of their ship from *Charles II* to the *Fancy* and set sail for the Indian Ocean. Along the way, they captured four other ships and made alliances with other pirates, so that by 1695, Avery had a virtual pirate army hunting for the ships that sailed between India and the Middle East.

The pirates knew there was an annual trade shipment that would be returning from Arabia back to India. The Indians would send shiploads of silk and spices to trade with the Arabians for gold, silver, and jewels. All the pirates had to do was wait.

Finally, one day, the pirates saw the fleet of ships over the horizon. But the Mughal ships saw the pirates. They broke up their convoy and the ships sailed in different directions. The pirate ships split up to chase them down.

Captain Avery and his crew first attacked the smaller ship, *Fateh Muhammed*. This crew saw the pirates and gave up without a fight. The pirates quickly took all of the food, cloth, and money they could find. They realized that the richer treasure was to be found on the larger ship that was sailing away.

Avery's ship, the *Fancy*, was smaller and faster than the large *Ganj-i-sawai*. They quickly overtook the Mughal ship and pulled alongside. The pirates boarded the ship, swinging cutlasses and firing their guns. This time, they were met with well-armed Moorish warriors. It was a bloody battle that left several dead on both sides, but in the end, Avery's crew took over the ship and ransacked it—looking for booty.

What they found amazed even Avery. The ship they captured was owned by the Grand Mughal and contained more than 600,000 pounds in gold, silver, and jewels. Each one of the surviving pirates received more than 1,000 pounds of the plunder. It was unimaginable wealth for sailors. They quickly loaded the goods back onto

the *Fancy* and set sail as fast as they could for the Caribbean. There the pirates felt they could sell their lie that they were just privateers and the authorities would not be as eager to chase them.

But pirates are not known for being good at keeping secrets. Several of the sailors bragged about their adventures and the authorities caught them and the pirates were hanged. Some of them tried to make their way back to England with their treasure. The authorities there were quite suspicious of sailors who were loaded with gold and silver. Many of those pirates were also caught, tried, and hanged.

The one pirate who seemed to be able to escape was Henry Avery. He told some of his sailors that he planned to live out his life in the Caribbean. He told others that he was going to England and still others that he would live out his life on the high seas. What he actually did is not known to historians. It seems he sailed for Ireland and then he simply disappeared. He is often considered the "successful pirate," because he knew when to stop thieving and how to keep his mouth shut. No one knows for sure if he settled down to be a wealthy landowner or if he died in poverty, but he was one of the few pirates that kept his head and his life.

The Scientist Pirate

William Dampier was the first person to sail around the world three times. He was an author, explorer, mapmaker, botanist, and zoologist. He was also a pirate who was convicted of cruelty.

Dampier was a smart man who liked studying science and nature and was excellent at navigation and map making. Born in 1697, he received his education at King's School in Bruton, England, and served in the British Royal Navy. But while he was working in the navy, he became seriously ill. He was discharged and returned to England, where it took several months before he was strong enough to work again.

For the next few years, Dampier stayed away from the sailing life. He tried his hand at working on a plantation in

Jamaica, but he didn't like farming. Next, he tried working as a logwood cutter in Central America. Logwood trees were used to produce red dye used in Europe for dyeing cloth. The trees grew on the edges of swamps, so Dampier and his fellow worker spent hours wading through swamps swatting mosquitos and watching for alligators. At night, they had to check their feet for worms that would burrow into their skin. They had to pull the worms out of their feet and legs so they didn't get infected.

After several months in the swamps, life on a ship started to look more inviting to Dampier and he joined a group of buccaneers. Life as a buccaneer meant sailing along the shore making raids on coastal villages. Dampier helped the buccaneers steal valuables, animals, and food.

After a few months with the buccaneers, Dampier decided that raiding was much easier than wading through swamps or working on a farm. He joined a group of pirates who were anchored by Jamaica and began hunting Spanish ships that were sailing from America back to Spain loaded with gold from the New World.

All the while Dampier was working, he was also writing. He kept a journal where he not only recorded the raids and battles, but also wrote about the people he encountered and the different trees, plants, and animals. He kept meticu-

lous records of tides, weather, and sailing conditions. He also drew maps of the coastline and the places he traveled. These journals would prove to be greater treasure than anything Dampier ever captured as a pirate.

In 1686, Dampier set off on his first voyage around the world. He joined the crew of the *Cygnet* on a 12-gun ship with a crew of 100 men. The ship was headed for the coast of Guam, but the crew had miscalculated the navigation. The ship's supplies were down to only 3 days of food and there was no land in sight. Some of the crew members made plans to kill the captain and use him for food.

Fortunately land was sighted. The captain was spared, and the crew was able to reload with supplies and water in the Philippines. They set off again and headed to the land they called New Holland, which was later named Australia. Dampier and the crew of pirates became the first Englishmen to set foot on the Australian continent, and Dampier's journal gave the English their first descriptions of Australian aborigines and the plants and animals of that continent.

When Dampier returned home, he published his journals. The people of Europe were fascinated with his stories of animals that hopped and carried their young in a pouch. They wanted to read about the tattooed people of the South Seas and the exotic plants and flowers of this strange new world. Dampier's book was incredibly popular, and Dampier became something of a celebrity.

The British Royal Navy believed such a great explorer should be given command of a ship and Dampier was made the captain of the *HMS Roebuck*. Unfortunately for the navy, Dampier was a much better scientist than he was a captain.

Dampier's mission was to explore the east coast of New Holland (Australia). It was a long voyage and full of arguments with his first lieutenant and some of the other sailors. When Dampier's ship reached Brazil, he had his lieutenant removed from the ship and put in jail.

Dampier sailed on and made it back to the west coast of Australia. Then with the help of his clerk, James Brand, he began making detailed drawings and descriptions of the plants and animals of the region. He also collected specimens to take back, including seeds, shells, and giant clams.

But the *Roebuck* was in bad condition. The ship's wood was rotting and in danger of sinking. Dampier had to abandon his plans and attempt to return to England. The ship never made it. The *Roebuck* sank in Ascension Bay. Dampier and his crew made a raft of boards and managed to make it to shore, where they were marooned for 5 weeks before they were rescued by an East Indian Company vessel and returned home.

Dampier managed to protect his precious journal and drawings by putting them in a length of bamboo and sealing the ends with wax. The journals, drawings, and a few samples were the only cargo that survived the trip.

When Dampier returned home, he was immediately court-martialed because he had jailed his lieutenant. He was convicted of "hard and cruel usage" and had to forfeit all of his pay. He was also deemed unfit to command any of His Majesty's ships.

But Dampier had become so famous because of his journals that a group of private ship owners hired Dampier to act as a privateer. This time his assignment was to attack and plunder as many Spanish ships as he could find and bring the gold and spoils back to England. The ship owners were sure that the famous pirate Dampier would make them wealthy.

But once again, Dampier got into arguments with his crew. He kicked his lieutenant off the ship. Then he kicked off another nine sailors. He lost every fight he had with another ship and never took any treasure. Dampier's crew was so disgusted with their captain that half of them deserted the ship at the next port. Dampier did eventually make it back to England, but it was a complete loss to the men who had invested in him and they were ready to sue him in court.

Lucky for Dampier, Captain Woodes Rogers knew that although Dampier may not be a good captain, he was excellent at navigation and knew more about the coast and islands of the South Seas than anyone else in the world. Captain Rogers hired Dampier on as pilot and navigator. This was a job much better suited to Dampier's skills. They set sail in 1708.

The voyage took 3 years and circled the globe. They fought Spanish galleons and won. They rescued Alexander Selkirk, who had been marooned on an island for 4 years. They brought back a huge treasure that gave each sailor a prize worth $100,000 in today's pay. It was also Dampier's last voyage. When they returned to England in 1711, Dampier was 60 years old. He retired from pirating and sailing and lived in a small cottage where he died 3 years later.

Dampier is still remembered as the first recorder of Australian flora and fauna. He is also cited more than 80 times in the Oxford English Dictionary because he introduced so many new words to the English language. He is credited with introducing such words as avocado, barbecue, breadfruit, cashew, catamaran, and chopsticks.

DAMPIER'S INFLUENCE

Dampier's journals were so widely read that nearly 150 later, scientist Charles Darwin took a copy of the journals on his famous trip to South America. The legendary explorer James Cook used Dampier's maps of winds and currents on his journeys. And Jonathan Swift, author of *Gulliver's Travels*, named one of his characters after Dampier.

Mary Read & Anne Bonny

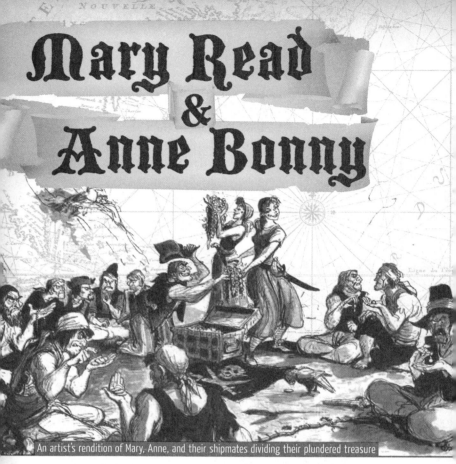

An artist's rendition of Mary, Anne, and their shipmates dividing their plundered treasure

Mary shifted from foot to foot, uncomfortable wearing a boy's breeches and coat. Her long hair had been shorn off, and her mother had given strict instructions that Mary was to stay quiet during the meeting with the old lady. Their future welfare depended on the old lady believing that Mary was her long-lost grandson.

In reality, Mary was the illegitimate child of Polly Read. Mary's mother had been married to Alfred Read when she gave birth to a baby boy. Alfred went out to sea and never returned. The boy died just a few months before the illegitimate Mary was born. Destitute without any way of earning a living, Mary's mother came up with an elaborate scheme to get money from her husband's family.

She would pretend that Mary was actually the dead son that had been born to her and Alfred. She presented Mary to Alfred's mother and begged for money to support the old woman's grandchild. The plan worked, and the grandmother agreed to send money every week to support her dear grandson. From that day on, Mary dressed as a boy.

When Mary was a teenager, the grandmother died and the weekly allowance stopped. Mary was force to go to work to support herself and her mother. Still dressed as a boy, she went to work as a footboy in a wealthy home. She soon became tired of working as a servant and decided to enlist in the military.

Mary served as both a foot soldier and in a horse regiment, all the while disguised as a man and giving her name as Mark Read. She served well and proved herself in battle, but she made one mistake. She fell in love with a fellow soldier. She finally admitted to the handsome Flemish soldier that she was a woman. They were married, and this time Mary wore a dress.

For the next few years, Mary was happy dressing as a woman and working with her husband at the inn they owned. But when Mary's husband became ill and died, she put back on her disguise and this time went to work as a sailor on a ship bound for the West Indies.

The sailing life agreed with Mary. She was a hard worker and liked the outdoors. She was settling in to her new occupation when her ship was attacked by pirates. The crew did not give much of a fight and the pirates took all of the goods they wanted, captured a few sailors, and then released the ship and its crew.

Mary was one of the sailors who was captured. She spent the next few months learning how to attack and capture ships. She seemed to be pretty good at it and was described by her fellow pirates as being fearless and the person who often led the raids.

Never afraid to give her opinion, Mary eventually disagreed with her captain. She joined a mutiny to get rid of the captain and ultimately changed ships. This time she went to work for the pirate known as Calico Jack Rackham.

Calico Jack got his name because of the flamboyant clothes he liked to wear. He especially loved coats made from Indian calico cloth. When Mary joined the crew, she had no idea that there was another woman aboard. Calico's Jack's girlfriend, Anne Bonny, sailed with his crew—also disguised as a man.

The two women eventually discovered each other's secret and became friends. Together, they were a formidable fighting team. As a teenager, Anne had run away from her father's plantation and married a pirate named James Bonny. After a short marriage, Anne and James were divorced, and Anne met Calico Jack.

Anne joined Calico Jack's crew and worked alongside the men. When Anne discovered that Mark Read was actually Mary Read, she informed Calico Jack. But unlike most pirate captains, Calico Jack didn't seem to have any problem with having women onboard his ship—just as long as they worked and fought as hard as the other men.

Calico Jack

But the life of crime caught up with the three pirates. In October of 1720, a pirate hunter named Jonathan Barnet surprised Calico Jack. The crew had been celebrating and was quite drunk. When Barnet's men attacked Calico Jack's ship, the only people willing to fight were Mary Read, Anne Bonny, and one other pirate. The women were furious that the men were not trying to defend their ship.

Mary was so angry that she shot down into the hold where her fellow pirates were hiding. She killed one man and wounded several others. They still didn't come up and fight. The whole crew was captured and taken to trial in Spanish Town, Jamaica. Calico Jack, Mary Read, Anne Bonny, and the rest of the crew were sentenced to hang. But at the trial, Mary and Anne stood before the court and "pleaded their bellies," meaning they claimed to be pregnant. It was against the law to hang pregnant women.

Mary and Anne were both given a temporary stay of execution until they gave birth. They were thrown into prison, where Mary contracted a violent fever and died. There is no historical record of Anne's release or her execution. It is believed that her wealthy father may have ransomed her, and she may have returned home with him. It is not known what happened to her child or if she was ever really pregnant.

CAPTAIN KIDD'S FATE

When pirates were caught and convicted, they knew they would hang. But hanging didn't scare pirates as much as the fate of Captain Kidd. When Kidd was hanged, the rope broke and he had to be strung up a second time to kill him. After he died, the magistrates had his body tarred to preserve it and then hung it in chains in the Thames estuary. It hung there for many years. Most pirates claimed they would rather blow themselves up that be "hang'd up a sun-drying" like Captain Kidd.

The Lonely Pirate

Alexander Selkirk was always in trouble. As a boy living in the small Scottish town of Fife, he got in trouble for fistfights and being disrespectful to his elders. He was opinionated and always ready to argue. And as the youngest of seven children, he had a lot of practice with arguments.

In 1693, he was called before the church elders to be disciplined for being disrespectful. Apparently the punishment didn't take. Just a few years later, he was sent to the church elders again—this time because his brother had played a prank on him. Alexander had been fooled into drinking seawater. He got so mad that he fought with two of his brothers, a sister-in-law, and his dad. This time, Alexander didn't even go to the church meeting. Instead, he ran away to sea and became a privateer—a pirate working for the king of England.

School was never Alexander's favorite place to be, but he was good at mathematics and geography. He used those skills to become a navigator. He learned to calculate the speed of the ship, the direction of the vessel, and to plot a course on a map. He was the sailor responsible for making changes to the direction the ship was going in order to keep the crew from being lost at sea. During the 1700s, the navigator depended on the stars, a compass, and mathematical calculations. Maps and sea charts were just becoming available, so a good navigator was extremely valuable to a sea captain.

In 1703, Alexander signed on with the privateer and explorer William Dampier and headed to the South Seas. Dampier carried letters of marque from the King of England. The letters of marque gave him permission to attack the enemy ships of England. Because this was during the War of the Spanish Succession, this meant Alexander and his shipmates would be attacking French and Spanish ships and looting them for all of the cargo and treasure they could steal. Privateer ships helped the English fight against their enemies without the expense of building Royal Navy boats or paying Royal Navy sailors. The privateers paid themselves with whatever they could steal and because they had a letter of marque, they were not supposed to be tried and hanged as pirates. Some countries went ahead and hanged privateers as pirates anyway, but at least they would not be tried in England.

Alexander was assigned to serve on the ship *Cinque Ports* as sailing master. This was a smaller ship that traveled with Dampier's crew of boats. The captain was Thomas Stradling. For more than a year, the ships worked under the direction of Captain Dampier. They attacked and raided Spanish ships and captured prizes of brandy, sugar, wine, and flour. They raided for gold and cargos of cloth, spices, and dyes. But after a year of sailing together, Thomas Stradling decided he could do better on his own and ordered his crew to go a different direction from Dampier.

This didn't sit well with Alexander. He felt that Stradling had too little experience to be a good captain and too little sense to know that his ship was badly in need of repair. When Stradling order the ship to stop at a small, uninhabited island off the coast of Chile, Alexander had enough. He argued with Stradling that they needed to stay at the island and make repairs to the ship. Stradling was sick of Alexander and all of his arguments, so when Alexander threatened to stay on the island if they didn't repair the ship, Stradling told him to stay.

Alexander found himself dumped on the deserted island with his clothes and a few tools, including his navigation tools. As the ship began to sail away, Alexander realized what a mistake he had made. None of the other sailors had agreed to stay with him. He was going to be left alone until another ship might stop at the island.

Alexander begged Stradling to take him back on the boat, but Stradling wanted to teach the rest of the crew a lesson. If they argued with him, there would be dire consequences. The *Cinque Ports* sailed off, and Alexander was left all by himself.

At first, Alexander was sure that there would be another ship stopping at the island in a few weeks. He stayed near the shore and watched the horizon. But weeks turned into months and there were no ships. Alexander was completely alone.

For more than 4 years, Alexander lived on the island with only animals for company. At first, he could not even sleep safely because rats would come out of the forest and gnaw on his hands and feet when he tried to sleep. He eventually was able to tame feral cats and they chased the rats away. He also tamed feral goats so he had goat's milk, meat, and leather. He built a home out of pepper trees, sewed clothes from goatskins, and spent time reading his Bible—all the while hoping and praying that one day a ship would arrive.

Unfortunately, the only two ships that stopped in 4 years were both Spanish. He knew that, as a Scotsman, if he were to be found by the Spanish, then he would be captured and either enslaved or tortured to death. The first time the Spanish arrived, he managed to stay hidden, but the second time some of the crew saw him. They chased Alexander through the forest, but he scrambled up a tree and (even though they walked right underneath it) they never found him.

Finally after 4 years and 4 months, two ships flying English flags sailed into the quiet island harbor. Alexander quickly lit a fire to attract the ships. A landing party was sent ashore to see what or who had built the fire. When the landing party arrived, they saw a man with matted long hair and a wild beard wearing goatskin pants. Alexander was so excited to see people, he could barely remember how to speak.

The captain and leader of the two ships was Woodes Rogers, and his assistant was none other than William Dampier, the captain Alexander had been serving under before the arrogant Stradling had taken over.

Dampier was amazed to see his former navigator alive. Dampier told Alexander that he had been right—Stradling's ship was not seaworthy and had sunk off the coast of Peru, killing all but Stradling and a dozen men. Stradling and the other survivors had been locked away in Spanish prisons or killed for being pirates.

Captain Rogers and his ships stayed for several weeks on the island, eating the fresh fruit and the goats supplied by Alexander. He served the sailors goat stew, and they gave him clothes and shoes. The shoes made his feet swell, so he just kept going barefoot. When it came time to leave, Alexander gladly boarded the ship and became a sailor again. He spent 2 more years at sea before he ever made it back to Scotland.

"Alexander Selkirk Makes His Cats and Kids Dance before Captn. Cook[e] and His Company." From Volume Two of David Henry's *An Historical Account of All the Voyages Round the World, Performed by English Navigators . . .* (1774)

When he arrived in Scotland, Alexander became something of a celebrity. Captain Rogers and Dampier had told newspapers about Alexander's 4 years of being marooned on an island. But although Alexander now had money and fame, he was not happy on land. He didn't like all of the attention. He said he was happier when he was worth nothing. After a few years, he returned to the life of a sailor. This time he was the first mate of a naval warship—the *HMS Weymouth*—headed to the Gold Coast of Africa looking for pirates. He never returned to land. He died of typhoid fever and was buried at sea.

Dice Game

Pirates and sailors often played dice games. You can have some pirate fun playing the game dice game Pig.

Materials:

☐ Two dice   ☐ Paper

☐ Pencil

The goal of this game is to be the first person to reach 100 and not go over.

The first player starts throwing the dice and can continue until he rolls a one or decides to stop throwing. When he throws the dice, he adds the numbers from each roll to his total. But if he rolls a one, he loses all of his points.

The problem is to know when to stop so you don't lose your new points.

Every time a player throws the dice, he adds the number to his total and if he stops before he rolls a one he can add to his grand total until he reaches 100. Go over 100 and you lose your points!

Player's Name	Points

Pirate Training

Make a Catapult

Launch a pirate attack with this simple-to-make catapult.

Materials:
- ❑ Seven craft sticks
- ❑ Four rubber bands
- ❑ Milk jug cap
- ❑ Cotton balls
- ❑ Glue

Stack five of the craft sticks together and rubber band them together on each end. Stack the other two craft sticks together and rubber band them together on one end.

Open the two craft sticks and insert the stack of five sticks inside. The two sticks will be propped open by the five sticks.

Wrap a rubber band around all of the craft sticks to hold them together. Then glue the milk cap to the top of one of the two craft sticks. This will be the catapult launching platform. Once it is dry, launch your cotton balls by pressing down on the top craft stick. Help your friends make their own catapult and you can have a cotton ball fight.

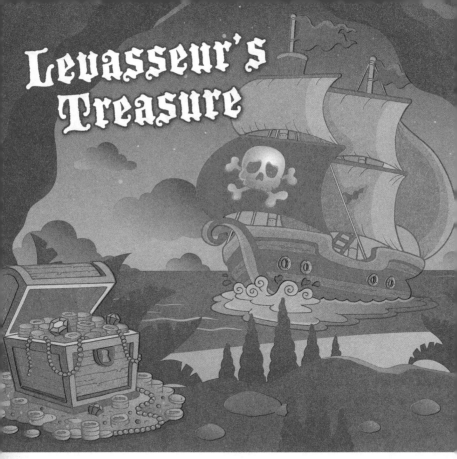

Levasseur's Treasure

    Although there is no record of any pirate leaving a treasure map, Olivier Levasseur left a treasure mystery that has never been solved.

    As a pirate, Levasseur was called "the buzzard" because of how fast and ruthless he was when he attacked his enemies. He was born to a wealthy family and sailed as a privateer for King Louis XIV of France during the War of the Spanish Succession. In 1716, when the war was over, he was supposed to return home with his ship, but instead he joined the pirate crew of Benjamin Hornigold.

    Although he had a scar across one eye, Levasseur proved to be a good leader and excellent sailor. Eventually he became captain of his own ship and partnered with two other pirate captains, Howell Davis and Thomas Cocklyn. Together they attacked ships on the West African coast.

Levasseur then partnered with pirate John Taylor, and they made one of piracy's greatest heists. They captured the Portuguese galleon *Our Lady of the Cape*. This large ship was full of gold, silver, diamonds, pearls, silk, and religious objects. The pirates found a gold cross that was inlaid with diamonds, rubies, and emeralds and was so heavy it took three men to lift it.

When the pirates divided the loot up among their crew, each pirate received 50,000 golden guineas. That would be more than $113 million in today's money! Each man was also given 42 diamonds. As was the pirate tradition, the two captains split the rest of the treasure and Levasseur took the golden cross.

In 1724, Levasseur tried to negotiate amnesty with the French government, but the French wanted Levasseur to turn over his treasure. Levasseur refused and lived in secret on the island of Bourbon off the coast of Africa.

In 1730, the French government found him and sentenced him to hang for piracy. Legend says that when Levasseur stood on the platform of the gallows he was wearing a necklace that contained a 17-line cryptogram (code). Just before he was hung, Levasseur threw the necklace into the crowd and said, "Find my treasure, the one who may understand it!"

For three centuries, treasure hunters have been trying to figure out the cryptogram and the location of the treasure. No one has been successful, but people are still trying.

CRACK LEVASSEUR'S CODE

This is a copy of Levasseur's cryptogram and his alphabet.
Could you be the person who finally finds his treasure?

À	Ċ	Ė	B	D	F
·G	I	K·	H	J	L
M	O	Q	N	P	R

A-	F-	K-	P-	U-
B-	G-	L-	Q-	V-
C-	H-	M-	R-	
D-	I-	N-	S-	
E-	J-	O-	T-	

Read more at http://en.wikipedia.org/wiki/Olivier_Levasseur

Spanish Gold

The ship was loaded with treasure: beautiful fabrics, exotic spices, and hundreds of pounds of gold and silver. In 1804, the *Nuestra Señora de las Mercedes* (Our Lady of Mercies) was on its way from South America to Portugal to deliver the goods to the Spanish government. The ship was escorted by three other Spanish frigates armed with defensive cannons. They were watching for pirates who might attack and rob the ship. What they didn't count on was being attacked by the British Navy.

As they sailed into the Cape of Santa Maria, they were surprised to be flagged down by a British ship and ordered to surrender. Spain and Britain were not officially at war and

$500 million worth of Spanish 'pieces of eight' coins found in a shipwreck must be returned to Spain

the Spanish commander refused to obey the order. The British ship fired a shot across the bow and the *Mercedes* responded. Cannonballs flew through the air and crashed into the hull of the *Mercedes*. Within a few moments, a huge explosion tore the ship apart, killing most of the sailors on board. The treasure sank to the bottom of the ocean floor.

The British captured the remaining three ships and confiscated their cargo of silver, gold, and jewels. The Spanish were furious, declaring it an act of war. The British claimed they had every right to intercept the ships because the money would have been used in wars to fight against England. For more than 200 years, the remainder of the treasure lay on the floor or the ocean out of reach of either England or Spain.

But in 2007, American underwater archeologists diving off the coast of Portugal found the remains of a sunken ship. In the ruins of the ship were thousands and thousands of silver and gold coins. It was a treasure haul that would have made Blackbeard jealous. The American divers salvaged 17 tons of coins and brought their findings back to the United States. It was estimated that the treasure was worth $500 million U.S. dollars.

But the American treasure hunters didn't get to enjoy their loot for long. As soon as the Spanish government heard about their find, they went to court and argued that because it came from a Spanish ship, it rightfully belonged to the country of Spain. In this court fight, it was not a case of "finders keepers." The courts ruled that Spain did have the right to the coins and the archaeologists had to give up their treasure trove.

Then the government of Peru got into the fight. They said that the gold and silver for the coins was actually stolen from

The sinking of the *Nuestra Señora de las Mercedes*

the mines of Peru. Spain shouldn't get the treasure; instead it should be given to the government of Peru. But the courts again decided in favor of Spain, explaining that in 1804 when the treasure was lost, Peru was actually a colony of Spain and not its own country.

In 2012, the Spanish government took over the treasure of the *Nuestra Señora de las Mercedes*. The whole treasure is being studied by the National Museum of Underwater Archaeology in Cartagena, Spain.

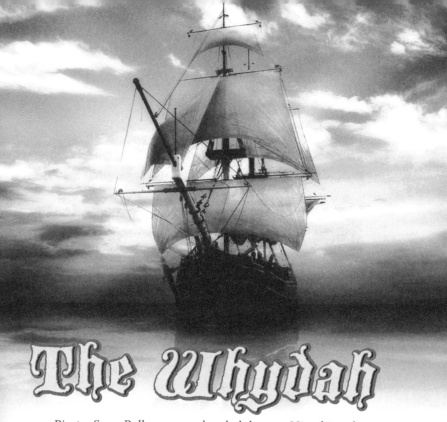

The Whydah

Pirate Sam Bellamy was headed home. His ship, the *Whydah*, was loaded with tons of silver, gold, guns, and treasure he had captured from his raids. All he had to do was to find a safe place to land on the coast of Massachusetts. Then Sam could be reunited with his girlfriend, Maria Hallet. They could get married and live a life of wealth beyond anyone's dreams. The only thing that stood between Sam and success was an April storm.

By April of 1717, Sam Bellamy had become one of the most successful pirates in history. He had captured at least 53 ships and enough treasure to make all of his crew members wealthy. He was known as Black Sam because he refused to wear the powdered wigs that were popular at the time; instead he grew his black hair long and tied it back in a simple band.

Legend says that Black Sam was a pirate with a purpose. The story goes that while Sam was working as a sailor along the coast of Cape Cod, he fell in love with a beautiful teenage girl, Maria Hallet. Her family disapproved of Maria marrying a poor sailor, so in 1716, Sam set out to sea to earn his fortune as a pirate. A little over a year later, Sam had a boatload of treasure and was headed back to Cape Cod and Maria.

But the night of April 26, there was a heavy fog covering the coast near the cliffs of Wellfleet. Sam was an experienced sailor and his crew knew how to manage a storm. They were close to a port they knew well and decided to take the risk. But the fog rolled and broiled and turned into a nasty nor'easter with winds whipping the sails at 70 mph. The ship was pummeled with 40-foot waves and a torrent of rain. At midnight, the main mast snapped and the *Whydah* capsized in 30 feet of water. The 60 cannons that were onboard ripped through the overturned decks and the ship was shattered. That night, Black Sam and his crew of 145 men went down with the ship. There were only two survivors.

Early the next morning, hundreds of Cape Cod's wreckers were scavenging for the remains of the ship and its treasure. The locals grabbed everything that they could from ship timbers and parts of sailcloth, to ropes and oars. The governor of Massachusetts ordered his own salvager to the scene hoping to recover some of the gold and silver.

But when salvage Captain Cyprian Southack arrived, there just wasn't much left. Everything that was floating had been scavenged by the locals. And Captain Southack correctly guessed that the heavy metal coins, guns, and munitions would be buried under water and sand. They did not have any diving technology, so there was no way to recover anything of value. Southack did make a map of the wreckage site, but there was no further effort to recover Black Sam's vast treasure. It lay at the bottom of the ocean—forgotten for more than 250 years.

Gold from the pirate ship *Whydah*

The bell, inscribed, "THE WHYDAH GALLY 1716" stowed in a water-filled vat to prevent drying displayed at Expedition *Whydah* Sea-Lab & Learning Center (The Whydah Pirate Museum) in Provincetown, MA

By the 1950s, most people thought that the story of Black Sam and his pirate treasure were just tall tales not to be taken seriously. Young Barry Clifford loved to listen to his uncle's stories of pirates like Black Sam. The wreck of the *Whydah* was Clifford's favorite tale. He dreamed that someday he would go diving and find the gold and silver that sank with the ship.

When Clifford went to college, he studied history and sociology. After college, he went to work learning about underwater construction, oil-spill control, and sea rescue and salvage. The entire time he kept thinking about the *Whydah*, wondering if it was really off the coast of Cape Cod. He began researching old maps from the 1700s. He studied the maps that Captain Southack had drawn in 1717. Clifford compared the shoreline of 1717 to the shoreline of the 1980s. The more he researched, the more Clifford became convinced that he could find the *Whydah* and Black Sam's treasure.

In 1982, Clifford's dream came true when he used his own money to fund an archaeological exploration team. With the help of more modern technology, they were able to find evidence of a shipwreck. They began pulling up cannonballs, lead shot, and gold coins. Clifford and his team were elated. Surely they had found the lost pirate treasure.

But other archaeologists were not sure it was the *Whydah*. It could have been one of many ships that had wrecked off the coast of Cape Cod. There needed to be some proof that this was Black Sam's ship. For 2 years, Clifford and his team carefully excavated the site and recovered more than 200,000 artifacts. Then, in 1984, they hit the jackpot—not a chest full of gold but an old ship's bell that was inscribed with the name *Whydah*. Clifford had proof that this was Black Sam's pirate ship. It was the first documented pirate ship to be recovered in the northern hemisphere.

Clifford became famous as an underwater archaeologist. He spent the next 30 years helping uncover lost shipwrecks in Panama, Belize, Venezuela, and the United States, but he always came back to his favorite ship, the *Whydah*.

In 2013, he led his team back to the site and they began digging deeper into the sand. They uncovered even more gold and silver. Clifford is sure that there is still treasure yet to be found and plans to keep digging until he can rescue all of Black Sam's treasure.

HOW MUCH LOST TREASURE IS THERE, REALLY?

Shipwrecks have been reported throughout history. From the ancient Greek and Roman ships to more modern tragedies like the sinking of the Titanic, some authorities estimate that there are more than a million ships under water now. That's the potential for a lot of treasure under the sea. Not every ship was carrying gold and silver, but many of them had valuable cargo. Some shipwreck hunters estimate that there is $60 **billion** worth of treasure lost at sea, just waiting for searchers to find it.

Oak Island Mystery

Legends of pirate treasure hidden in caves and buried on islands are still believed by treasure hunters today. The real truth is that most of the treasure that is recovered is from ships that sank in the ocean. But one island treasure story has fascinated fortune hunters for more than two centuries. It is the mystery of Oak Island and it still has not been solved.

Stories were told of treasure hoards buried by Captain Kidd or Blackbeard off the coast of Nova Scotia. Everyone believed it was the stuff of pure imagination until one day in 1795, when a teenager, Daniel McGinnis, went exploring on Oak Island. He claimed to have seen lights on the island and wanted to know what they were, so he rowed over during daylight and started searching the island.

He didn't see any shipwrecked sailors, but he did find a strange circular depression in a clearing on the southern side of the island. Next to the strange spot in the ground was a tree gouged with the type of groove that would result from using a tackle block to hoist up heavy loads. McGinnis got excited. Maybe this was the place where Captain Kidd had hidden his treasure? He went home and came back with friends. Armed with shovels, they began excavating the circular depression.

They quickly discovered that the hole was definitely man-made. They could see evidence of pick axe marks on the walls of the hole. They also found layers of logs every 10 feet and flagstones. What was the purpose of this tunnel? It had obviously been built by someone for a reason. McGinnis and his friends were sure they would hit a treasure trove if they could just dig deep enough. But it was getting dark and they only had a couple of shovels. They realized that they would need better tools and more people. They made a pact to return one day and finish their treasure hunt.

It was 9 years before the men returned to the site. This time, they came prepared. They had hired local laborers to help with the dig. Everyone involved was working for a share of the treasure. They dug down 59 feet and found traces of coconut fibers. Coconuts were not native to Nova Scotia. They were a tropical plant and would have had to have been hauled in by someone. Could it have been Captain Kidd or Blackbeard?

Excited, the men kept digging. They found an oak platform and more oak board sealed with putty. Then a shovel hit something hard. They carefully lifted out a smooth stone that had carving on it. It was in code that no one understood. Surely this was the marker for the treasure!

The men dug deeper and found more wood, but no treasure. By now, it was night and too dark to keep digging. The entire party decided to stop and return the next morning. They were certain they would reach the end of the tunnel then.

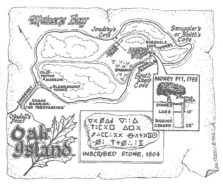

The next morning, the treasure hunters were met with a terrible sight: the hole had filled with seawater. All of their work was flooded. They tried to pump the water out of the hole, but it kept refilling. They tried to dig a shaft next to the hole, but it caved in on them. They were lucky to escape with their lives.

For the next 200 years, treasure hunters tried at various times to excavate the deep tunnels on Oak Island. Diggers have found that there is more than one tunnel. Not only that, but the original tunnel seems to have a booby trap that the first diggers triggered—what flooded the tunnel. Professional treasure hunters and archaeologists have continued the search for the truth of the Oak Island tunnel, but it still remains a mystery.

Who built the elaborate tunnel and what does it hide? Is there any treasure on the island or was it taken years ago? It is a treasure mystery still waiting to be solved!

Franklin D. Roosevelt, pictured above, was part of the Old Gold Salvage group of 1909 and kept up with news and developments for most of his life

WHAT LIES BENEATH OAK ISLAND? AND WHY?

Theories abound as to why the Oak Island pit, which became known as the "Money Pit," was actually built. Many believe that it was built as a secret vault to hid pirate treasure, but others think that the pit might be much older and could have been built by Vikings or native people who lived on the islands before Europeans arrived. Was it used as a burial tomb or treasure vault? It's going to take more digging and exploration to learn the truth.

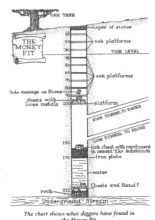

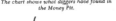

The chart shows what diggers have found in the Money Pit.

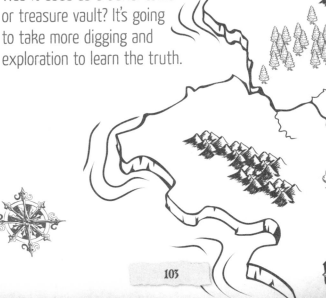

Make a Treasure Map

Pirates may not have made treasure maps, but they did use maps to sail their ships. They also made maps of islands and coasts they visited. They used the maps to help them hide out from their enemies.

You can create a map to show where you have hidden a treasure or a safe place to hide out.

Materials:

- ❑ Paper
- ❑ Pencil
- ❑ A friend
- ❑ Candy

First, decide where you want your hiding place to be. You can either hide a small treasure there—like a candy bar—or you can hide yourself. If you are hiding yourself, you can tell your friend that this is your new pirate hideout.

Use the paper below to draw a picture of your hiding place. Put that in the center of the paper. Think about all of the objects around that hiding place and draw pictures of them. Try to give clues to your friend. For example, if you are hiding in your bedroom, draw your bed. Use your imagination and get creative.

Give the map to your friend and challenge him or her to see if he or she can find your secret hiding place. If he or she finds you, then you might want to reward him or her with that candy bar!

My Treasure Map

Make Your Own Compass

One of the tools a pirate used to help in navigation was a compass. You can build your own compass and tell which way your pirate ship is headed.

Materials:

- ❏ Magnet
- ❏ Cork
- ❏ Large needle
- ❏ Straight pin

- ❏ Shallow dish at least 9 inches in diameter
- ❏ Compass

Magnetize the needle by rubbing it, in one direction only, with one pole of the magnet. Test the magnetized needle by trying to pick up a straight pin with the needle. If you can pick up the pin, your needle is ready.

Push the needle through the cork so that the needle is laying horizontal to the table.

Fill the dish with water. Place the cork with the needle into the dish so that the cork floats in the center. The magnetized needle will point toward north. You can check to see if your compass works by setting a manufactured compass next to it.

Once you have made your compass, use it to draw a map of your house and show which direction your house faces. Is the front door in the north, south, east, or west? Is your room on the north or south side of the house?

Bibliography

Books

Cordingly, D. (1995). *Under the black flag: The romance and the reality of life among the pirates.* New York, NY: Random House.

Cordingly, D. (1996). *Pirates: Terror on the high seas from the Caribbean to the South China Sea.* Atlanta, GA: Turner Publishing.

Cordingly, D. (2011). *Pirate hunter of the Caribbean.* New York, NY: Random House.

Gosse, P. (1990). *The history of piracy.* Glorieta, NM: The Rio Grande Press.

Gosse, P. (1988). *The pirates' who's who.* Glorieta, NM: The Rio Grande Press.

Johnson, C. (2010). *A general history of the robberies and murders of the most notorious pirates.* New York, NY: Lyons Press. (Original work published 1725)

Konstam, A. (2007). *Pirates: Predators of the seas.* New York, NY: Skyhorse Publishing.

Sherry, F. (1986). *Raiders and rebels: The golden age of piracy.* New York, NY: Hearst Marine Books.

Woodard, C. (2008). *The republic of pirates: Being the true and surprising story of the Caribbean pirates and the man who brought them down.* New York, NY: Harcourt.

Websites

Barry Clifford, undersea explorer. (n.d.). Retrieved from http://www.western.edu/profile/alumnus/barry-clifford-undersea-explorer

Bruno, J. (n.d.). *Sadie the Goat: The queen of the waterfront.* Retrieved from http://joebrunoonthemob.wordpress.com/2012/02/12/joe-bruno-on-the-mob-sadie-the-goat-the-queen-of-the-waterfront/

Cavendish, R. (2001). Execution of Captain Kidd. *History Today.* Retrieved from http://www.historytoday.com/richard-cavendish/execution-captain-kidd

Clendenning, A. (2012). Nuestra Senora de las Mercedes treasure shown for the first time. *The World Post.* Retrieved from http://www.huffingtonpost.com/2012/11/30/nuestra-senora-de-las-mercedes-treasure_n_2217132.html

Decayeux, A. (n.d.). *The pirate flag & the Jolly Roger.* Retrieved from http://www.pirates-privateers.com/pirate-flag-jolly-roger.htm

Drye, W. (2011). Blackbeard's ship confirmed off North Carolina. *National Geographic News.* Retrieved from http://news.nationalgeographic.com/news/2011/08/11 0829-blackbeard-shipwreck-pirates-archaeology-science/

Easy and fun catapult for kids to make. (2013). *Kids Activities Blog.* Retrieved from http://kidsactivitiesblog.com/28871/catapult-for-kids-to-make

Famous people Dampier influenced. (n.d.). Retrieved from http://ocean.si.edu/ocean-news/famous-people-dampier -influenced

Goodier, R. (2012). What's the total value of the world's sunken treasure? *Popular Mechanics.* Retrieved from http:// www.popularmechanics.com/technology/infrastruc ture/a7425/whats-the-total-value-of-the-worlds-sunken-treasure/

Is pirate treasure lost 300 years ago in shipwreck buried at the end of a 'yellow brick road' on the bottom of the sea? (2013). *Daily Mail.* Retrieved from http://www.dailymail. co.uk/news/article-2432319/Whydah-Gally-Is-pirate-treasure-lost-300-years-ago-shipwreck-the-sea.html

Mancini, M. (2014). 11 rules from an actual pirate code. *Mental_Floss.* Retrieved from http://mentalfloss.com/ article/58900/11-rules-actual-pirate-code

MassMoments.org. (n.d.). *Explorer proves wreck is Whydah.* Retrieved from http://www.massmoments.org/moment. cfm?mid=313

Melina, R. (2011). Why did pirates wear earrings? *Live Science.* Retrieved from http://www.livescience.com/33099-why-did-pirates-wear-earrings-.html

The mystery pit of Oak Island. (n.d.). Retrieved from http:// www.unmuseum.org/oakisl.htm

Oak Island treasure: History. (n.d.). Retrieved from http:// www.oakislandtreasure.co.uk/content/section/5/35/

Ossian, R. (n.d.). *Pirate weaponry.* Retrieved from http:// www.thepirateking.com/historical/weapons.htm

Ossian, R. (n.d.). *Cheng I Sao.* Retrieved from http://www. thepirateking.com/bios/sao_cheng_i.htm

Staley, J. (n.d.). *Grace O'Malley.* Retrieved from http://www. rootsweb.ancestry.com/~nwa/grace.html

Wikipedia. (n.d.). *Ching Shih.* Retrieved from http://en.wiki pedia.org/wiki/Ching_Shih

Wikipedia. (n.d.). *Sadie Farrell.* Retrieved from http://en.wiki
    pedia.org/wiki/Sadie_Farrell

Wikipedia. (n.d.). *Jeanne de Clisson.* Retrieved from http://en.
    wikipedia.org/wiki/Jeanne_de_Clisson

Wikipedia. (n.d.). *Jolly Roger.* Retrieved from http://en.wiki
    pedia.org/wiki/Jolly_Roger

Wikipedia. (n.d.). *Oak Island.* Retrieved from http://en.wiki
    pedia.org/wiki/Oak_Island

Wikipedia. (n.d.). *Olivier Levasseur.* Retrieved from http://en.
    wikipedia.org/wiki/Olivier_Levasseur

Wikipedia. (n.d.). *Pirate code.* Retrieved from http://en.wiki
    pedia.org/wiki/Pirate_code

About the Author

Stephanie Bearce is a writer, a teacher, and a history detective. She loves tracking down spies and uncovering secret missions from the comfort of her library in St. Charles, MO. When she isn't writing or teaching, Stephanie loves to travel the world and go on adventures with her husband, Darrell.

More Books in This Series

Stealthy spies, secret weapons, and special missions are just part of the mysteries uncovered when kids dare to take a peek at the *Top Secret Files*. Featuring books that focus on often unknown aspects of history, this series is sure to hook even the most reluctant readers, taking them on a journey as they try to unlock some of the secrets of our past.

Top Secret Files: The American Revolution
George Washington had his own secret agents, hired pirates to fight the British, and helped Congress smuggle weapons, but you won't learn that in your history books! Learn the true stories of the American Revolution and how spies used musket balls, books, and laundry to send messages. Discover the female Paul Revere, solve a spy puzzle, and make your own disappearing ink. It's all part of the true stories from the *Top Secret Files: The American Revolution*.
ISBN-13: 978-1-61821-247-4

Top Secret Files: The Civil War
The Pigpen Cipher, the Devil's Coffee Mill, and germ warfare were all a part of the Civil War, but you won't learn that in your history books! Discover the truth about Widow Greenhow's spy ring, how soldiers stole a locomotive, and the identity of the mysterious "Gray Ghost." Then learn how to build a model submarine and send secret light signals to your friends. It's all part of the true stories from the *Top Secret Files: The Civil War*.

ISBN-13: 978-1-61821-250-4

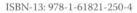

Top Secret Files: The Cold War
Poison dart umbrellas, lipstick pistols, and cyanide guns were all a part of the arsenal of tools used by spies of the Soviet KGB, American CIA, and British MI6, but you won't learn that in your history books! Discover how East Germans tried to ride zip lines to freedom, while the Cambridge Four infiltrated Britain and master spy catchers like Charles Elwell were celebrated. Then make your own secret codes and practice sending shoe messages. It's all part of the true stories from the *Top Secret Files: The Cold War*.
ISBN-13: 978-1-61821-419-5 • **Available August 2015**

Top Secret Files: Gangsters and Bootleggers

Blind pigs, speakeasies, coffin varnish, and tarantula juice were all a part of the Roaring 20s. Making alcohol illegal didn't get rid of bars and taverns or crime bosses—they just went underground. Secret joints were in almost every large city. Discover the crazy language and secret codes of the Prohibition Era—why you should mind your beeswax and watch out for the gumshoe talking to the fuzz or you might end up in the cooler! It's all part of the true stories from the *Top Secret Files: Gangsters and Bootleggers*.

ISBN-13: 978-1-61821-461-4 • **Available October 2015**

Top Secret Files: The Wild West

Bandits, lawmen, six shooters, bank robberies, and cowboys were all a part of the Wild West. But so were camels, buried treasure, and gun-slinging dentists. Dive into strange tales like the mysterious Cave of Gold, filled with ancient skeletons, and Rattle Snake Dick's lost fortune. Discover the truth about notorious legends like Jesse James, Buffalo Bill, former spy-turned-bandit Belle Star, and Butch Cassidy and the Sundance Kid. Then, learn why it's unlucky to have a dead man's hand when playing cards and how to talk like a real cowpoke. It's all part of the true stories from the *Top Secret Files: The Wild West*.

ISBN-13: 978-1-61821-462-1 • **Available October 2015**

Top Secret Files: World War I

Flame throwers, spy trees, bird bombs, and Hell Fighters were all a part of World War I, but you won't learn that in your history books! Uncover long-lost secrets of spies like Howard Burnham, "The One Legged Wonder," and nurse-turned-spy, Edith Cavell. Peek into secret files to learn the truth about the Red Baron and the mysterious Mata Hari. Then learn how to build your own Zeppelin balloon and mix up some invisible ink. It's all part of the true stories from the *Top Secret Files: World War I*.

ISBN-13: 978-1-61821-241-2

Top Secret Files: World War II

Spy school, poison pens, exploding muffins, and Night Witches were all a part of World War II, but you won't learn that in your history books! Crack open secret files and read about the mysterious Ghost Army, rat bombs, and doodlebugs. Discover famous spies like the White Mouse, super-agent Garbo, and baseball player and spy, Moe Berg. Then build your own secret agent kit and create a spy code. It's all part of the true stories from the *Top Secret Files: World War II*.

ISBN-13: 978-1-61821-244-3